CW00551315

MAN CAVE COOKING

Publications International, Ltd.

Photographs on front cover copyright © Shutterstock.com.

Pictured on the front cover *(clockwise from top left):* Chili Cheese Fries *(page 41)*, Classic Grilled Burgers *(page 127)*, Bold and Zesty Beef Back Ribs *(page 141)*, Soft Pretzel Bites *(page 42)* and Buffalo Chicken Wings *(page 18)*.

Pictured on the back cover *(clockwise from top left):* Ice Cream Pizza Treat *(page 172)*, Mole Chili *(page 70)* and French Dip Sandwiches *(page 102)*.

ISBN: 978-1-64558-671-5

Manufactured in China.

8 7 6 5 4 3 2 1

Note: Hot peppers such as jalapeño peppers, serrano peppers and habanero peppers can sting and irritate the skin, so wear rubber gloves when handling peppers and do not touch your eyes.

Microwave Cooking: Microwave ovens vary in wattage. Use the cooking times as guidelines and check for doneness before adding more time.

Let's get social!
 @Publications_International

@PublicationsInternational

www.pilbooks.com

CONTENTS

BOOZE & BREWS

‹ BRANDY COLLINS

2 ounces brandy

1 ounce lemon juice

1 teaspoon powdered sugar

3 ounces chilled club soda

Orange slice and
maraschino cherry

Fill cocktail shaker half full with ice; add brandy, lemon juice and powdered sugar. Shake until blended; strain into ice-filled Collins glass. Add club soda; stir until blended. Garnish with orange slice and maraschino cherry.

MAKES 1 SERVING

SAZERAC

2 ounces whiskey

¼ ounce anise-flavored
liqueur

½ ounce simple syrup*

Dash of bitters

*To make simple syrup,
combine 1 part water
and 1 part sugar in small
saucepan. Cook over medium
heat until sugar is dissolved,
stirring frequently. Cool to
room temperature; store in
glass jar in refrigerator.*

Fill cocktail shaker half full with ice; add whiskey, liqueur, syrup and bitters. Stir until blended; strain into old fashioned glass.

MAKES 1 SERVING

MICHELADA CUBANA ›

1 lime wedge

Coarse salt

2 tablespoons lime juice

1 teaspoon Worcestershire sauce

1 teaspoon hot pepper sauce

½ teaspoon Maggi seasoning or soy sauce

6 ounces chilled Mexican pale lager

Rub rim of beer glass with lime wedge; dip in salt. Fill glass with ice; add lime juice, Worcestershire sauce, hot pepper sauce and Maggi seasoning. Top with beer.

MAKES 1 SERVING

CUBA LIBRE

2 ounces rum

Chilled cola

Lime wedge

Fill chilled highball glass half full with ice. Pour rum over ice; fill with cola. Garnish with lime wedge.

MAKES 1 SERVING

EL DORADO

2 ounces tequila

1 tablespoon honey

1½ ounces lemon juice

Lemon or orange slice

Fill cocktail shaker half full with ice; add tequila, honey and lemon juice. Shake until blended; strain into ice-filled old fashioned or Collins glass. Garnish with lemon slice.

MAKES 1 SERVING

JACK ROSE ›

- 2 ounces applejack
- ¾ ounce lime juice
- ¾ ounce grenadine
- Lime slice or wedge

Fill cocktail shaker half full with ice; add applejack, lime juice and grenadine. Shake about 15 seconds or until cold; strain into chilled cocktail glass or coupe. Garnish with lime slice.

MAKES 1 SERVING

MOJITO

- 8 fresh mint leaves, plus additional for garnish
- 2 ounces lime juice
- 2 teaspoons superfine sugar or powdered sugar
- 3 ounces light rum
- Soda water
- 2 lime slices

Combine half of mint leaves, lime juice and sugar in each of two highball glasses; mash with wooden spoon or muddler. Fill glass with ice. Pour rum over ice; top with soda water. Garnish with lime slices and remaining mint.

MAKES 2 SERVINGS

BOULEVARDIER

- 1½ ounces bourbon
- 1 ounce sweet vermouth
- 1 ounce Campari
- Orange slice or twist

Fill mixing glass or cocktail shaker half full with ice; add bourbon, vermouth and Campari. Stir 30 seconds or until cold; strain into chilled old fashioned or cocktail glass. Garnish with orange slice.

MAKES 1 SERVING

GIN AND TONIC ›

2 ounces gin

4 ounces tonic water

Green grape (optional)

Lime wedge

Fill old fashioned glass with ice; pour gin over ice. Stir in tonic water. Garnish with grape and lime wedge.

MAKES 1 SERVING

OLD FASHIONED

1 sugar cube*

2 dashes Angostura bitters

1 teaspoon water

2 ounces whiskey

Lemon peel twist

Or use 2 teaspoons simple syrup. Stir together simple syrup, bitters and water in glass.

Place sugar cube, bitters and water in old fashioned glass; muddle until sugar is dissolved. Fill glass half full with ice; stir in whiskey and lemon twist.

MAKES 1 SERVING

CUBAN BEER SPRITZER

3 cups (24 ounces) cold beer (pilsner or pale ale)

3 cups (24 ounces) cold ginger ale

½ cup lime juice

⅓ cup sugar

2 cups crushed ice

Lime slices

Combine beer, ginger ale, lime juice and sugar in large pitcher; stir until sugar is dissolved. Fill glasses with crushed ice; pour in spritzer. Garnish with lime slices.

MAKES 4 TO 6 SERVINGS

MARTINEZ ›

1½ ounces gin
¾ ounce sweet vermouth
½ ounce maraschino liqueur
2 dashes orange bitters
Lemon or orange twist

Fill mixing glass with ice; add gin, vermouth, liqueur and bitters. Stir about 20 seconds or until very cold; strain into chilled coupe or cocktail glass. Garnish with lemon twist.

MAKES 1 SERVING

NEGRONI

1 ounce gin
1 ounce Campari
1 ounce sweet or dry vermouth
Orange slice or twist

Fill cocktail shaker half full with ice; add gin, Campari and vermouth. Stir until blended; strain into chilled cocktail glass. Garnish with orange slice.

MAKES 1 SERVING

RUSTY NAIL

1½ ounces Scotch
1 ounce Drambuie

Stir together Scotch and Drambuie in ice-filled old fashioned glass.

MAKES 1 SERVING

SNAKE BITE ›

8 ounces ale

8 ounces hard cider

Pour ale into chilled pint glass; top with cider. (Do not stir.)

MAKES 1 SERVING

HALF-AND-HALF

8 ounces ale

8 ounces porter

Pour ale into chilled pint glass. Pour porter over back of spoon on top of ale. (Do not stir.)

MAKES 1 SERVING

BRAVE BULL

1½ ounces tequila

1 ounce coffee liqueur

Lemon twist

Fill chilled old fashioned glass with ice; add tequila and liqueur. Stir until blended; garnish with lemon twist.

MAKES 1 SERVING

BAR BITES

CHICKEN BACON QUESADILLAS

4 teaspoons vegetable oil, divided

4 (8-inch) flour tortillas

1 cup (4 ounces) shredded Colby-Jack cheese

2 cups coarsely chopped cooked chicken

4 slices bacon, crisp-cooked and coarsely chopped

½ cup pico de gallo, plus additional for serving

Sour cream and guacamole (optional)

1. Heat large nonstick skillet over medium heat; brush with 1 teaspoon oil. Place one tortilla in skillet; sprinkle with ¼ cup cheese. Spread ½ cup chicken over one half of tortilla; top with one fourth of bacon and 2 tablespoons pico de gallo.

2. Cook 1 to 2 minutes or until cheese is melted and bottom of tortilla is lightly browned. Fold tortilla over filling, pressing with spatula. Transfer to cutting board; cool slightly. Cut into wedges. Repeat with remaining ingredients.

3. Serve with additional pico de gallo, sour cream and guacamole, if desired.

MAKES 4 SERVINGS

BUFFALO CHICKEN WINGS

1 cup hot pepper sauce

⅓ cup vegetable oil, plus additional for frying

1 teaspoon sugar

½ teaspoon ground red pepper

½ teaspoon garlic powder

½ teaspoon Worcestershire sauce

⅛ teaspoon black pepper

1 pound chicken wings, tips discarded, separated at joints

Blue cheese or ranch dressing

Celery sticks

1. Combine hot pepper sauce, ⅓ cup oil, sugar, red pepper, garlic powder, Worcestershire sauce and black pepper in small saucepan; cook over medium heat 20 minutes. Pour sauce into large bowl.

2. Heat 3 inches of oil in large saucepan over medium-high heat to 350°F; adjust heat to maintain temperature during frying. Add wings; cook 10 minutes or until crispy. Drain on wire rack set over paper towels.

3. Transfer wings to bowl of sauce; toss to coat. Serve with blue cheese dressing and celery sticks.

MAKES 4 SERVINGS

MAC AND CHEESE BITES

- 3 tablespoons butter, divided
- 2 tablespoons all-purpose flour
- 1 cup milk
- 1 teaspoon salt
- ½ teaspoon black pepper
- 1 cup (4 ounces) shredded sharp Cheddar cheese
- 1 cup (4 ounces) shredded Muenster cheese
- ½ pound elbow macaroni, cooked and drained
- ⅓ cup panko or plain dry bread crumbs

    Finely chopped fresh parsley (optional)

1. Preheat oven to 400°F. Melt 1 tablespoon butter in large saucepan over medium heat; grease 36 mini (1¾-inch) muffin cups with melted butter.

2. Melt remaining 2 tablespoons butter in same saucepan over medium heat. Whisk in flour; cook and stir 2 minutes. Add milk, salt and pepper; cook and stir 3 minutes or until thickened. Remove from heat; gradually stir in cheeses. Fold in macaroni. Divide mixture among prepared muffin cups; sprinkle with panko.

3. Bake about 25 minutes or until golden brown. Cool in pans 10 minutes; remove carefully using sharp knife. Garnish with parsley.

MAKES 36 APPETIZERS

MOZZARELLA STICKS

¼ cup all-purpose flour

2 eggs

1 tablespoon water

1 cup plain dry bread crumbs

2 teaspoons Italian seasoning

½ teaspoon salt

½ teaspoon garlic powder

1 package (12 ounces) string cheese (12 sticks)

Vegetable oil for frying

1 cup marinara or pizza sauce, heated

1. Place flour in shallow bowl. Whisk eggs and water in another shallow bowl. Combine bread crumbs, Italian seasoning, salt and garlic powder in third shallow bowl.

2. Coat each piece of cheese with flour. Dip in egg mixture, letting excess drip back into bowl. Roll in bread crumb mixture to coat. Dip again in egg mixture and roll again in bread crumb mixture. Place on plate or baking sheet; refrigerate until ready to cook.

3. Heat 2 inches of oil in large saucepan over medium-high heat to 350°F; adjust heat to maintain temperature during frying. Add cheese sticks in batches; cook about 1 minute or until golden brown. Drain on wire rack. Serve with warm marinara sauce for dipping.

MAKES 12 STICKS

BARBECUE CHICKEN PIZZA

1 pound refrigerated pizza dough

1 tablespoon olive oil

6 ounces boneless skinless chicken breasts, cut into strips (about 2×¼ inch)

¼ teaspoon salt

⅛ teaspoon black pepper

6 tablespoons barbecue sauce, divided

⅔ cup shredded mozzarella cheese, divided

½ cup shredded smoked Gouda cheese, divided

½ small red onion, cut vertically into ⅛-inch slices

2 tablespoons chopped fresh cilantro

1. Preheat oven to 450°F. Line baking sheet with parchment paper. Let dough come to room temperature.

2. Heat oil in large skillet over medium-high heat. Season chicken with salt and pepper; cook about 5 minutes or just until cooked though, stirring occasionally. Remove chicken to medium bowl. Add 2 tablespoons barbecue sauce; stir to coat.

3. Roll out dough into 12-inch circle on lightly floured surface. Transfer to prepared baking sheet. Spread remaining 4 tablespoons barbecue sauce over dough, leaving ½-inch border. Sprinkle with 2 tablespoons mozzarella cheese and 2 tablespoons Gouda cheese. Top with chicken and onion; sprinkle with remaining cheeses.

4. Bake 12 to 15 minutes or until crust is browned and cheese is bubbly. Sprinkle with cilantro just before serving.

MAKES 4 SERVINGS

BEER-BRAISED MEATBALLS

1   pound ground beef

½   cup seasoned dry bread crumbs

½   cup grated Parmesan cheese

2   eggs, lightly beaten

⅓   cup finely chopped onion

2   cloves garlic, minced

½   teaspoon black pepper

¼   teaspoon salt

1   bottle (12 ounces) lager or other light-colored beer

1½ cups tomato sauce

1   cup ketchup

2   tablespoons tomato paste

½   cup packed brown sugar

1. Preheat oven to 400°F. Line baking sheet with foil; spray with nonstick cooking spray.

2. Combine beef, bread crumbs, cheese, eggs, onion, garlic, pepper and salt in large bowl; mix gently but thoroughly. Shape mixture into 1-inch balls. Place meatballs on prepared baking sheet. Bake 10 minutes or until browned.

3. Combine beer, tomato sauce, ketchup, tomato paste and brown sugar in Dutch oven; bring to a boil over medium-high heat. Add meatballs. Reduce heat to medium-low; cover and simmer 20 to 30 minutes or until meatballs are cooked through, stirring occasionally.

MAKES 20 MEATBALLS

CHEESY GARLIC BREAD

- 1 loaf (about 16 ounces) Italian bread
- ½ cup (1 stick) butter, softened
- 8 cloves garlic, very thinly sliced
- ¼ cup grated Parmesan cheese
- 2 cups (8 ounces) shredded mozzarella cheese

1. Preheat oven to 425°F. Line large baking sheet with foil.

2. Cut bread in half horizontally. Spread cut sides of bread evenly with butter; top with sliced garlic. Sprinkle with Parmesan cheese, then mozzarella cheese. Place on prepared baking sheet.

3. Bake 12 minutes or until cheeses are melted and golden brown in spots. Cut crosswise into slices. Serve warm.

MAKES 8 TO 10 SERVINGS

DUO OF MINI CHEESEBURGERS

½ pound ground turkey

1 teaspoon chili powder

½ teaspoon salt, divided

½ pound ground beef

2 tablespoons minced onion

¼ teaspoon black pepper

2 tablespoons salsa

1 tablespoon hickory-flavored barbecue sauce

4 slices Cheddar or American cheese, halved diagonally

8 small whole wheat dinner rolls or slider rolls, split and lightly toasted

1. Preheat broiler. Line baking sheet with foil.

2. Combine turkey, chili powder and ¼ teaspoon salt in medium bowl; mix well. Shape into four patties about 3 inches in diameter and ½ inch thick. Combine beef, onion, remaining ¼ teaspoon salt and pepper in separate medium bowl; mix well.

Shape into four patties. Place all patties on prepared baking sheet.

3. Broil patties 4 minutes per side or until no longer pink in center. Spoon salsa over turkey patties and barbecue sauce over beef patties; top all patties with cheese. Broil 1 minute or until cheese is melted. Serve in rolls.

MAKES 4 SERVINGS (8 SLIDERS)

CHICKEN IN A BLANKET

1 package (about 11 ounces) refrigerated breadstick dough (8 count)

1 package (10 ounces) Italian-seasoned cooked chicken breast strips

Ketchup, mustard and/or barbecue sauce

1. Preheat oven to 375°F. Line baking sheet with parchment paper or foil.

2. Unroll dough on cutting board; separate into individual breadsticks. Pat or roll out each breadstick to 7×1½-inch rectangle (¼ inch thick); half crosswise to form 16 pieces total.

3. Cut chicken strips in half crosswise. Place one piece of chicken on each piece of dough; wrap dough around chicken and seal, pressing edges together tightly. Place seam side down on prepared baking sheet.

4. Bake 15 to 17 minutes or until light golden brown. Decorate with ketchup, mustard and/or barbecue sauce. Serve warm with additional sauces for dipping.

MAKES 16 BITES

BAKED BEER-BATTERED ONIONS AND SHRIMP

4 tablespoons vegetable oil

1 large sweet onion

1 cup all-purpose flour, divided

1 teaspoon salt, divided

¾ teaspoon ground red pepper, divided

½ cup lager or other light-colored beer

1 egg

1½ cups panko or regular bread crumbs

¼ teaspoon black pepper

1 pound large shrimp, cleaned, peeled and deveined

Dipping sauce: ketchup, barbecue sauce, ranch dressing and/or cocktail sauce (optional)

1. Preheat oven to 425°F. Spread 2 tablespoons vegetable oil on each of two large baking sheets.

2. Slice onion into ½-inch circles and separate into rings, keeping only large whole rings (reserve remaining onion for another use).

3. Combine ¾ cup flour, ½ teaspoon salt and ½ teaspoon ground red pepper in medium bowl; mix well. Beat lager and egg in small bowl; stir into flour mixture.

4. Combine panko, remaining ¼ cup flour, remaining ½ teaspoon salt, remaining ¼ teaspoon ground red pepper and black pepper in resealable food storage bag. Dredge onion slices in batter; place in bag and shake to coat. Spread on one prepared baking sheet. Repeat with shrimp and place on second baking sheet.

5. Bake onion rings 8 minutes. Turn rings over and bake 8 minutes. Bake shrimp on top rack 5 minutes; turn and bake 5 minutes. Serve hot with dipping sauce, if desired.

MAKES 4 TO 6 SERVINGS

SWEET AND SPICY BEER NUTS

2 cups pecan halves

2 teaspoons salt

2 teaspoons chili powder

2 teaspoons olive oil

½ teaspoon ground cumin

¼ teaspoon ground red pepper

½ cup sugar

½ cup beer

1. Preheat oven to 350°F. Line baking sheet with foil.

2. Mix pecans, salt, chili powder, oil, cumin and ground red pepper in small bowl. Spread on prepared baking sheet. Bake 10 minutes or until fragrant, stirring frequently. Cool on baking sheet on wire rack.

3. Combine sugar and beer in small saucepan. Heat over medium-high heat until mixture registers 250°F on candy thermometer. Remove from heat; carefully stir in nuts and any loose spices. Spread sugared nuts on baking sheet, separating clusters.

4. Let cool completely. Break up any large pieces before serving.

MAKES 3 CUPS

CHIPOTLE CHICKEN QUESADILLAS

- 1 package (8 ounces) cream cheese, softened
- 1 cup (4 ounces) shredded Mexican cheese blend
- 1 tablespoon minced canned chipotle pepper in adobo sauce
- 5 (10-inch) flour tortillas
- 5 cups shredded cooked chicken (about 1¼ pounds)
- Optional toppings: guacamole, sour cream, salsa and/or chopped fresh cilantro

1. Combine cream cheese, Mexican cheese blend and chipotle pepper in large bowl; mix well.

2. Spread ⅓ cup cheese mixture over half of one tortilla. Top with about 1 cup chicken. Fold tortilla over filling and press gently. Repeat with remaining tortillas, cheese mixture and chicken.

3. Heat large nonstick skillet over medium-high heat. Add two quesadillas; cook 2 to 3 minutes per side or until lightly browned.

4. Cut each quesadilla into four wedges. Serve with desired toppings.

MAKES 5 SERVINGS

GAME-ON GRUB

CHILI CHEESE FRIES

1½ pounds ground beef

1 medium onion, chopped

2 cloves garlic, minced

1 can (about 14 ounces) diced tomatoes

2 tablespoons chili powder

2 tablespoons tomato paste

½ teaspoon salt

¼ teaspoon black pepper

1 package (32 ounces) frozen French fries

1 jar (15 ounces) nacho cheese or cheese sauce, heated

Sour cream, chopped green onions and shredded Cheddar cheese or Mexican cheese blend (optional)

1. Brown beef, onion and garlic in large skillet over medium-high heat 6 to 8 minutes, stirring to break up meat. Drain fat.

2. Stir tomatoes, chili powder, tomato paste, salt and pepper into beef mixture. Simmer 20 minutes or until most liquid has evaporated, stirring occasionally.

3. Meanwhile, bake French fries according to package directions.

4. Divide French fries evenly among serving bowls. Top evenly with nacho cheese and chili. Garnish with sour cream, green onions and shredded cheese.

MAKES 4 SERVINGS

SOFT PRETZEL BITES

HONEY-MUSTARD DIP

- ¾ cup sour cream
- ¼ cup Dijon mustard
- 3 tablespoons honey

PRETZEL BITES

- 1⅔ cups warm water (110° to 115°F)
- 1 package (¼ ounce) active dry yeast
- 2 teaspoons sugar
- ½ teaspoon fine salt
- 4½ cups all-purpose flour, plus additional for work surface
- 2 tablespoons butter, softened
- 2 tablespoons vegetable oil
- 12 cups water
- ½ cup baking soda
  Kosher or pretzel salt (optional)

1. For honey-mustard dip, stir sour cream, mustard and honey in small bowl until smooth and well blended. Cover; refrigerate until ready to serve.

2. For pretzels, whisk 1⅔ cups warm water, yeast, sugar and fine salt in large bowl. Let stand 5 minutes or until bubbly.

3. Add 4½ cups flour and butter to yeast mixture; beat with electric mixer at low speed until combined. Replace paddle attachment with dough hook. Beat at medium speed 5 minutes.

4. Spray large bowl with nonstick cooking spray. Place dough in bowl; turn to grease top. Cover and let rise in warm place 1 hour or until doubled in size.

5. Preheat oven to 450°F. Grease two large baking sheets with 1 tablespoon oil each.

6. Punch down dough; place on floured work surface. Cut dough into 12 equal pieces. Roll each piece into 12-inch-long rope. Cut each rope into eight equal pieces.

7. Bring 12 cups water to a boil in large saucepan. Stir in baking soda until dissolved. Working in batches, drop dough pieces into boiling water; boil 30 seconds. Remove to prepared baking sheets using slotted spoon.

8. Sprinkle pieces evenly with kosher salt. Bake 12 minutes or until dark golden brown, rotating baking sheets halfway through. Serve with honey-mustard dip.

MAKES 12 SERVINGS

CHICKEN FAJITA NACHOS

- 2 tablespoons vegetable oil, divided
- 2 red bell peppers, cut into thin strips
- 1 large onion, cut in half and thinly sliced
- 2 tablespoons fajita seasoning mix (from 1¼-ounce package), divided
- 2 tablespoons water, divided
- 1 large boneless skinless chicken breast (about 12 ounces), cut into 2×1-inch strips
- 4 cups tortilla chips (about 30 chips)
- ½ cup (2 ounces) shredded Cheddar cheese
- ½ cup (2 ounces) shredded Monterey Jack cheese
- 1 jalapeño pepper, seeded and thinly sliced
- 1 cup shredded lettuce
- ½ cup salsa
  Sour cream and guacamole (optional)

1. Heat 1 tablespoon oil in large skillet over medium-high heat. Add bell peppers and onion; cook 5 minutes or until tender and browned in spots, stirring frequently. Transfer to large bowl; stir in 1 tablespoon fajita seasoning mix and 1 tablespoon water.

2. Heat remaining 1 tablespoon oil in same skillet over medium-high heat. Add chicken; cook 7 to 10 minutes or until cooked through, stirring occasionally. Add remaining 1 tablespoon fajita seasoning mix and 1 tablespoon water; cook and stir 3 to 5 minutes or until chicken is coated.

3. Preheat broiler. Spread chips in 11×7-inch baking pan; top with vegetables, chicken, Cheddar cheese, Monterey Jack cheese and jalapeño pepper.

4. Broil 2 to 4 minutes or until cheeses are melted. Top with lettuce and salsa; serve with sour cream and guacamole, if desired.

MAKES 4 SERVINGS

PEPPERONI BREAD STICKS

1 package (about 14 ounces) refrigerated pizza dough

8 slices provolone cheese

20 to 30 slices pepperoni (about half of 6-ounce package)

½ teaspoon Italian seasoning

¾ cup (3 ounces) shredded mozzarella cheese

½ cup grated Parmesan cheese

1 egg, beaten

Marinara sauce, heated

1. Preheat oven to 400°F. Line baking sheet with parchment paper. Unroll pizza dough on parchment paper with long side facing you. Cut off corners of dough to create oval shape.

2. Arrange half of provolone slices over right half of dough, cutting to fit as necessary. Top with pepperoni; sprinkle with ¼ teaspoon Italian seasoning. Top with mozzarella cheese, Parmesan cheese and remaining provolone slices; sprinkle with remaining ¼ teaspoon Italian seasoning.

3. Fold top left half of dough over filling; press edges with fork or pinch edges to seal. Brush top with beaten egg.

4. Bake about 16 minutes or until crust is golden brown. Remove to wire rack to cool slightly. Cut crosswise into slices; serve warm with marinara sauce.

MAKES ABOUT 6 SERVINGS

SPICY KOREAN CHICKEN WINGS

2 tablespoons peanut oil, plus additional for frying

2 tablespoons grated fresh ginger

½ cup soy sauce

¼ cup cider vinegar

¼ cup honey

¼ cup chili garlic sauce

2 tablespoons orange juice

1 tablespoon dark sesame oil

18 chicken wings (wing tips removed) or drummettes

Sesame seeds (optional)

1. Heat 2 tablespoons peanut oil in medium skillet over medium-high heat. Add ginger; cook and stir 1 minute. Add soy sauce, vinegar, honey, chili garlic sauce, orange juice and sesame oil; cook and stir 2 minutes. Place sauce in large bowl.

2. Heat 2 inches of peanut oil in large heavy saucepan over medium-high heat to 350° to 375°F; adjust heat to maintain temperature.

3. Carefully add wings to oil and cook 8 to 10 minutes or until crispy and browned and chicken is cooked through. Remove to paper towel-lined plate to drain.

4. Add wings to sauce; toss to coat. Sprinkle with sesame seeds, if desired.

MAKES 6 TO 8 SERVINGS

SPICY BBQ PARTY FRANKS

- 1 tablespoon butter
- 1 package (1 pound) cocktail franks
- ⅓ cup cola
- ⅓ cup ketchup
- 2 tablespoons hot pepper sauce
- 2 tablespoons packed dark brown sugar
- 1 tablespoon cider vinegar

1. Melt butter in medium skillet over medium heat. Add franks to skillet; cook until lightly browned.

2. Stir in cola, ketchup, hot pepper sauce, brown sugar and vinegar. Reduce heat to low; cook until sauce is reduced to sticky glaze.

MAKES 6 TO 8 SERVINGS

BACON-WRAPPED DATES

1 container (12 ounces) whole Medjool dates

4 ounces goat cheese or blue cheese

1 pound thick-cut bacon (about 12 slices)

1. Preheat oven to 450°F. Line shallow baking pan or rimmed baking sheet with parchment paper.

2. Cut dates open on one side (do not cut all the way through dates); remove pits. Spoon about ½ teaspoon goat cheese in center of each date; close dates.

3. Cut bacon slices into halves. Wrap half slice of bacon around each date; secure with toothpick. Arrange dates 1-inch apart in prepared pan.

4. Bake 16 to 18 minutes or until bacon is crisp, turning once.

MAKES 8 TO 10 SERVINGS

LOADED TEX-MEX NACHOS

1 tablespoon vegetable oil

8 ounces ground beef

½ cup chopped onion

2 cloves garlic, minced

2 teaspoons chili powder

1 teaspoon ground cumin

½ teaspoon salt

½ teaspoon dried oregano

1 can (about 15 ounces) kidney beans, rinsed and drained

½ cup corn

½ cup sour cream, divided

2 tablespoons mayonnaise

1 tablespoon lime juice

¼ to ½ teaspoon chipotle chili powder

½ (11- to 12-ounce) bag tortilla chips

½ (15-ounce) jar nacho cheese or Cheddar cheese dip, warmed

½ cup pico de gallo

¼ cup guacamole

1 cup shredded iceberg lettuce

2 jalapeño peppers, thinly sliced into rings

1. Heat oil in large skillet over medium-high heat. Add beef, onion and garlic; cook and stir 6 to 8 minutes or until beef is no longer pink. Add chili powder, cumin, salt and oregano; cook and stir 1 minute. Add beans and corn; reduce heat to medium-low and cook 3 minutes or until heated through.

2. For chipotle sauce, combine ¼ cup sour cream, mayonnaise, lime juice and chipotle chili powder in small bowl; mix well. Place in small plastic squeeze bottle.

3. Spread tortilla chips on platter or large plate. Top with beef mixture; drizzle with cheese dip. Top with pico de gallo, guacamole, remaining ¼ cup sour cream, lettuce and jalapeño peppers. Squeeze chipotle sauce over nachos. Serve immediately.

MAKES 4 TO 6 SERVINGS

BEER DOUGH PEPPERONI PIZZA

1 cup lager or pale ale, at room temperature

3 tablespoons olive oil

1 package (¼ ounce) instant yeast

2¾ cups bread flour, plus additional for rolling dough

1 teaspoon salt

1 cup prepared pizza sauce

20 to 30 slices pepperoni (about half of 6-ounce package)

2 cups (8 ounces) shredded mozzarella cheese

¼ cup grated Parmesan cheese

1. Combine lager, oil and yeast in large bowl. Stir in 1 cup flour and salt. Gradually stir in enough flour to make thick dough. Knead on floured work surface 8 minutes or until smooth, adding flour as necessary to prevent sticking. Or knead with stand mixer fitted with dough hook on medium-low speed 5 to 7 minutes. Shape dough into a ball.

2. Spray large bowl with nonstick cooking spray. Place dough in bowl; turn to grease top. Cover with plastic wrap and let rise in warm place about 1 hour or until doubled in size.

3. Preheat oven to 425°F.

4. Divide dough in half; shape into two balls and place on lightly floured work surface. Cover with plastic wrap; let stand 10 minutes. Roll out one ball into 10-inch round. Transfer to ungreased baking sheet. Spread with ½ cup pizza sauce, leaving ½-inch border around edge. Top with half of pepperoni, 1 cup mozzarella cheese and 2 tablespoons Parmesan cheese. Repeat with remaining ingredients.

5. Bake 15 minutes or until crust is golden brown and cheeses are bubbly. Let stand 3 minutes before serving.

MAKES 2 (10-INCH) PIZZAS

MINI CHEESE DOGS

1 package (16 ounces) hot dogs (8 hot dogs)

6 ounces pasteurized process cheese product

2 packages (16 ounces each) jumbo homestyle buttermilk biscuits (8 biscuits per package)

1. Preheat oven to 350°F. Line baking sheet with parchment paper or spray with nonstick cooking spray.

2. Cut each hot dog into four pieces. Cut cheese into 32 (1×½-inch) pieces.

3. Separate biscuits; cut each biscuit in half. Wrap 1 piece of hot dog and 1 piece of cheese in each piece of dough; press ends of dough to seal. Place seam side up on prepared baking sheet.

4. Bake 15 minutes or until biscuits are golden brown. Serve warm.

MAKES 32 MINI CHEESE DOGS

WHITE SPINACH QUESO

1 tablespoon olive oil

1 clove garlic, minced

1 tablespoon all-purpose flour

1 can (12 ounces) evaporated milk

½ teaspoon salt

2 cups (8 ounces) shredded Monterey Jack cheese, divided

1 package (10 ounces) frozen chopped spinach, thawed and squeezed dry

Optional toppings: pico de gallo, guacamole, chopped fresh cilantro and queso fresco

Tortilla chips

1. Preheat broiler.

2. Heat oil in medium saucepan over medium-low heat. Add garlic; cook and stir 1 minute without browning. Add flour; whisk until smooth. Add evaporated milk in thin steady stream, whisking constantly. Stir in salt. Cook about 4 minutes or until slightly thickened, whisking frequently. Add 1½ cups Monterey Jack cheese; whisk until smooth. Stir in spinach. Pour into medium cast iron skillet; sprinkle with remaining ½ cup Monterey Jack cheese.

3. Broil about 1 minute or until cheese is melted and browned in spots. Top with pico de gallo, guacamole, cilantro and queso fresco, if desired. Serve immediately with tortilla chips.

MAKES 4 TO 6 SERVINGS

BAKED SALAMI

1 (32-ounce) all-beef kosher salami

1 jar (12 ounces) chili sauce

1½ cups water

¼ cup packed brown sugar
  Bread slices

1. Preheat oven to 325°F. Peel off plastic wrap and outer skin of salami. Cut 12 crosswise (½-inch-deep) slits across top.

2. Combine chili sauce, water and brown sugar in baking dish; stir well. Place salami in dish, cut side up. Spoon some of sauce over top.

3. Bake 1½ hours or until sauce has thickened and salami is dark brown, spooning sauce over salami every 20 minutes.

4. Cut salami into thin slices; toss with sauce. Serve with bread.

MAKES ABOUT 10 SERVINGS

CHILI COOK-OFF

FIVE-WAY CINCINNATI CHILI

- 1 pound uncooked spaghetti, broken in half
- 1 pound ground beef
- 2 cans (10 ounces each) tomatoes with green chiles, undrained
- 1 can (about 15 ounces) red kidney beans, drained
- 1 can (10½ ounces) condensed French onion soup, undiluted
- 1¼ cups water
- 1 tablespoon chili powder
- 1 teaspoon sugar
- ½ teaspoon salt
- ¼ teaspoon ground cinnamon
- ½ cup chopped onion
- ½ cup (2 ounces) shredded Cheddar cheese

1. Cook pasta in large saucepan of boiling salted water according to package directions until tender; drain.

2. Meanwhile, brown beef in large saucepan or Dutch oven over medium-high heat 6 to 8 minutes, stirring to break up meat; drain well. Add tomatoes, beans, soup, water, chili powder, sugar, salt and cinnamon to saucepan; bring to a boil. Reduce heat to low. Simmer, uncovered, 10 minutes, stirring occasionally.

3. Serve chili over spaghetti; sprinkle with onion and cheese.

MAKES 6 SERVINGS

CHILI WITH TURKEY AND BEANS

1 **pound ground turkey**

2 **cans (about 15 ounces each) red kidney beans, rinsed and drained**

2 **cans (about 14 ounces each) whole tomatoes, drained**

1 **can (about 15 ounces) black beans, rinsed and drained**

1 **can (12 ounces) tomato sauce**

1 **cup chopped onion**

1 **cup chopped celery**

1 **cup chopped carrots**

3 **tablespoons chili powder**

1 **tablespoon Worcestershire sauce**

4 **teaspoons ground cumin**

1 **teaspoon salt**

½ **teaspoon ground red pepper**

½ **cup amaretto (optional)**

Shredded Cheddar cheese

Cornbread (optional)

SLOW COOKER DIRECTIONS

1. Brown turkey in large skillet over medium-high heat, stirring to break up meat. Drain; place turkey in slow cooker.

2. Add kidney beans, tomatoes, black beans, tomato sauce, onion, celery, carrots, chili powder, Worcestershire sauce, cumin, salt, ground red pepper and amaretto, if desired; stir to blend.

3. Cover; cook on HIGH 7 hours. Top with cheese. Serve with cornbread, if desired.

MAKES 6 SERVINGS

CORN CHIP CHILI

1 tablespoon olive oil

1 medium onion, chopped

1 medium red bell pepper, chopped

1 jalapeño pepper, seeded and finely chopped

4 cloves garlic, minced

2 pounds ground beef

1 can (4 ounces) diced green chiles, drained

2 cans (about 14 ounces each) fire-roasted diced tomatoes

2 tablespoons chili powder

1½ teaspoons ground cumin

1½ teaspoons dried oregano

¾ teaspoon salt

3 cups corn chips

1 cup (4 ounces) shredded sharp Cheddar cheese

6 tablespoons chopped green onions

SLOW COOKER DIRECTIONS

1. Heat oil in large skillet over medium-high heat. Add onion, bell pepper, jalapeño pepper and garlic; cook and stir 3 minutes or until softened. Add beef; cook and stir 10 to 12 minutes or until beef is no longer pink and liquid has evaporated.

2. Stir in green chiles; cook 1 minute. Transfer beef mixture to slow cooker. Stir in tomatoes, chili powder, cumin, oregano and salt.

3. Cover; cook on LOW 6 to 7 hours or on HIGH 3 to 3½ hours. Place corn chips evenly into serving bowls; top with chili. Sprinkle with cheese and green onions.

MAKES 6 SERVINGS

MOLE CHILI

- 2 corn tortillas, each cut into 4 wedges
- 1½ pounds boneless beef chuck, cut into 1-inch pieces
- ¾ teaspoon salt
- ½ teaspoon black pepper
- 3 tablespoons olive oil, divided
- 2 medium onions, chopped
- 5 cloves garlic, minced
- 1 cup beef broth
- 1 can (about 14 ounces) fire-roasted diced tomatoes
- 2 tablespoons chili powder
- 1 tablespoon ground ancho chile
- 1 teaspoon ground cumin
- 1 teaspoon dried oregano
- ¾ teaspoon ground cinnamon
- 1 can (about 15 ounces) red kidney beans, rinsed and drained
- 1½ ounces semisweet chocolate, chopped
- Queso fresco and chopped fresh cilantro (optional)

SLOW COOKER DIRECTIONS

1. Place tortillas in food processor or blender; process to fine crumbs. Set aside.

2. Season beef with salt and pepper. Heat 1 tablespoon oil in large skillet over medium-high heat. Add half of beef; cook 4 minutes or until browned. Remove to slow cooker. Repeat with 1 tablespoon oil and remaining beef.

3. Heat remaining 1 tablespoon oil in skillet. Add onions and garlic; cook and stir 2 minutes or until starting to soften. Pour broth into skillet, scraping up any browned bits from bottom of skillet. Pour into slow cooker. Stir in reserved tortilla crumbs, tomatoes, chili powder, ancho chile, cumin, oregano and cinnamon.

4. Cover; cook on LOW 8 hours. Stir in beans. Cover; cook on LOW 30 minutes. Turn off heat. Add chocolate; stir until chocolate is melted. Top with queso fresco and cilantro, if desired.

MAKES 4 TO 6 SERVINGS

FOUR-BEAN CHILI

- 2 tablespoons olive oil
- 1 onion, finely chopped
- 2 medium carrots, chopped
- 1 red bell pepper, chopped
- ¼ cup tomato paste
- 3 tablespoons chili powder
- 2 tablespoons ground cumin
- 2 tablespoons packed dark brown sugar
- 3 cloves garlic, minced
- 1 tablespoon dried oregano
- 1 teaspoon salt
- 1 can (28 ounces) diced tomatoes
- 2 cups water
- 1 can (about 15 ounces) small white beans, rinsed and drained
- 1 can (about 15 ounces) light kidney beans, rinsed and drained
- 1 can (about 15 ounces) dark kidney beans, rinsed and drained
- 1 can (about 15 ounces) pinto beans, rinsed and drained
- 1 can (4 ounces) diced mild green chiles
- 1 ounce unsweetened baking chocolate, chopped
- 1 tablespoon cider vinegar

1. Heat oil in large saucepan or Dutch oven over medium-high heat. Add onion, carrots and bell pepper; cook 10 minutes or until vegetables are tender, stirring frequently. Add tomato paste, chili powder, cumin, brown sugar, garlic, oregano and salt; cook and stir 1 minute.

2. Stir in tomatoes, water, beans, chiles and chocolate; bring to a boil. Reduce heat to medium; simmer 20 minutes, stirring occasionally. Stir in vinegar.

MAKES 8 TO 10 SERVINGS

TEX-MEX CHILI

4 slices bacon, diced

2 pounds boneless beef top round or chuck shoulder steak, trimmed and cut into ½-inch cubes

1 medium onion, chopped

2 cloves garlic, minced

¼ cup chili powder

1 teaspoon salt

1 teaspoon dried oregano

1 teaspoon ground cumin

½ to 1 teaspoon ground red pepper

½ teaspoon hot pepper sauce

4 cups water

Additional chopped onion (optional)

1. Cook bacon in Dutch oven over medium-high heat until crisp. Drain on paper towel-lined plate.

2. Add half of beef to drippings in Dutch oven; cook and stir until lightly browned. Remove beef to plate; repeat with remaining beef.

3. Add onion and garlic to Dutch oven; cook and stir over medium heat 5 minutes or until onion is tender. Return beef and bacon to Dutch oven. Stir in chili powder, salt, oregano, cumin, red pepper and hot pepper sauce; mix well. Stir in water; bring to a boil over high heat.

4. Reduce heat to low; cover and simmer 1½ hours. Skim fat from surface; simmer, uncovered, 30 minutes or until beef is very tender and chili has thickened slightly. Garnish with additional chopped onion.

MAKES 6 SERVINGS

HOME-STYLE CHILI

1 pound ground beef

¾ cup chopped onion

½ teaspoon black pepper

¼ teaspoon salt

2 cans (about 14 ounces each) diced tomatoes with green chiles

1 can (15 ounces) chili beans in sauce

1 cup water

1 package (1¼ ounces) chili seasoning mix

2 cups (8 ounces) shredded Cheddar cheese

1. Brown beef in large skillet over medium-high heat 6 to 8 minutes, stirring to break up meat. Drain fat.

2. Add onion, pepper and salt; cook and stir 5 minutes or until onion is tender.

3. Stir in tomatoes, beans with sauce, water and seasoning mix; simmer 25 minutes, stirring occasionally. Divide among bowls; sprinkle with cheese.

MAKES 4 TO 6 SERVINGS

WHITE BEAN CHICKEN CHILI

- 1 tablespoon vegetable oil
- 1 pound ground chicken
- 3 cups chopped celery
- 1½ cups coarsely chopped onions
- 3 cloves garlic, minced
- 4 teaspoons chili powder
- 1½ teaspoons ground cumin
- ¾ teaspoon ground allspice
- ¾ teaspoon ground cinnamon
- ½ teaspoon salt
- ½ teaspoon black pepper
- 1 can (about 14 ounces) diced tomatoes
- 1 can (about 15 ounces) Great Northern beans, rinsed and drained
- 2 cups chicken broth

1. Heat oil in large skillet over medium heat. Add chicken; cook 6 to 8 minutes or browned, stirring to break up meat. Transfer chicken to bowl.

2. Add celery, onions and garlic to skillet; cook and stir over medium heat 5 to 7 minutes or until tender.

Sprinkle with chili powder, cumin, allspice, cinnamon, salt and pepper; cook and stir 1 minute.

3. Return chicken to skillet. Stir in tomatoes, beans and broth; bring to a boil. Reduce heat to low. Simmer, uncovered, 15 minutes.

MAKES 6 SERVINGS

CHILI VERDE

1 pound pork shoulder, cut into 1-inch cubes

1 large onion, halved and thinly sliced

6 cloves garlic, chopped or sliced

½ cup water

1 pound fresh tomatillos

1 can (about 14 ounces) chicken broth

1 can (4 ounces) diced mild green chiles, drained

1 teaspoon ground cumin

1 can (about 15 ounces) Great Northern beans, rinsed and drained

½ cup lightly packed fresh cilantro, chopped

Sliced jalapeño peppers (optional)

1. Place pork, onion, garlic and water in large saucepan. Cover; simmer over medium-low heat 30 minutes, stirring occasionally (add more water if necessary). Uncover; boil over medium-high heat until liquid evaporates and meat browns.

2. Stir in tomatillos and broth. Cover; simmer over medium heat 20 minutes or until tomatillos are tender. Pull tomatillos apart with two forks. Add chiles and cumin.

3. Cover; simmer over medium-low heat 45 minutes or until meat is tender and pulls apart easily. (Add more water or broth, if necessary, to keep liquid at same level.) Add beans; simmer 10 minutes or until heated through. Stir in cilantro. Top with jalapeño peppers, if desired.

MAKES 4 SERVINGS

GRILLED STEAK CHILI

¼ cup minced garlic

¼ cup corn oil

3 cups chopped onions

3 cans (about 14 ounces each) Mexican-style diced tomatoes with chiles

2 cans (about 14 ounces each) crushed tomatoes

2 cups beef broth

¼ cup plus 2 tablespoons chili powder

2 teaspoons ground cumin

2 teaspoons dried oregano

1 teaspoon salt

1 teaspoon black pepper

4 pounds beef steak (preferably rib-eye)

¼ cup masa harina (corn flour) or yellow cornmeal (optional)

Minced fresh cilantro and sliced green onions (optional)

1. Combine garlic and oil in Dutch oven over low heat; cook 1 minute. Add onions; cook and stir over medium heat 5 minutes. Stir in tomatoes, broth, chili powder, cumin, oregano, salt and pepper; bring to a boil, stirring occasionally. Reduce heat; cover and simmer 1 to 2 hours or until thick.

2. Preheat grill or broiler. Grill steak about 8 minutes or just until browned on both sides. Let stand 15 minutes.

3. Cut steak into 2×½-inch strips on rimmed cutting board. Stir steak and accumulated juices into chili; cook 5 to 10 minutes. For thicker chili, slowly add masa harina; cook and stir 12 to 15 minutes or until thickened. Garnish with cilantro and green onions.

MAKES 10 TO 12 SERVINGS

HEARTY CHICKEN CHILI

1 onion, finely chopped

1 jalapeño pepper, minced

1 clove garlic, minced

1½ teaspoons chili powder

¾ teaspoon salt

½ teaspoon ground cumin

½ teaspoon dried oregano

½ teaspoon black pepper

¼ teaspoon red pepper
   flakes (optional)

1½ pounds boneless skinless
   chicken thighs, cut into
   1-inch pieces

2 cans (about 15 ounces
   each) hominy, rinsed
   and drained

1 can (about 15 ounces)
   pinto beans, rinsed and
   drained

1 cup chicken broth

1 tablespoon all-purpose
   flour (optional)

   Chopped fresh cilantro or
   parsley (optional)

SLOW COOKER DIRECTIONS

1. Combine onion, jalapeño pepper, garlic, chili powder, salt, cumin, oregano, black pepper and red pepper flakes, if desired, in slow cooker.

2. Add chicken, hominy, beans and broth; mix well. Cover; cook on LOW 7 hours.

3. For thicker chili, stir 1 tablespoon flour into 3 tablespoons cooking liquid in small bowl. Stir into slow cooker. *Turn slow cooker to HIGH.* Cover; cook 10 minutes or until thickened. Garnish with cilantro.

MAKES 6 SERVINGS

BEEF CHUCK CHILI

3 tablespoons olive oil

5 pounds boneless beef chuck roast, trimmed

3 cups minced onions

4 poblano peppers,* diced

2 serrano peppers,* diced

2 green bell peppers, diced

3 jalapeño peppers, seeded and minced

2 tablespoons minced garlic

1 can (28 ounces) crushed tomatoes

4 ounces Mexican lager (optional)

¼ cup hot pepper sauce

1 tablespoon ground cumin

Cornbread (store bought or homemade; see recipes on pages 94–98)

*If fresh poblano or serrano peppers are unavailable, use 2 cans (4 ounces each) diced green chiles, adding chili powder for more heat.

SLOW COOKER DIRECTIONS

1. Heat oil in large skillet over medium-high heat. Add roast; brown on all sides. Transfer to slow cooker.

2. Add onions, peppers and garlic to skillet; cook and stir 5 minutes or until onions are tender. Transfer to slow cooker. Stir in crushed tomatoes. Cover; cook on LOW 4 to 5 hours.

3. Remove beef to cutting board; shred with two forks. Return shredded beef to slow cooker. Stir in beer, if desired, hot pepper sauce and cumin. Serve over cornbread.

MAKES 8 TO 10 SERVINGS

BEER-BRAISED CHILI

2 tablespoons canola or vegetable oil

2 pounds boneless beef chuck roast or stew meat, cut into ¾-inch cubes

1 large onion, chopped

4 cloves garlic, minced

1 tablespoon chili powder

1 tablespoon ground cumin

1¼ teaspoons salt

1 teaspoon dried oregano

½ teaspoon ground red pepper

1 can (about 14 ounces) Mexican-style stewed tomatoes, undrained

1 bottle or can (12 ounces) light-colored beer

½ cup salsa

1 can (about 15 ounces) black beans, rinsed and drained

1 can (about 15 ounces) red beans or pinto beans, rinsed and drained

Optional toppings: chopped fresh cilantro, sliced green onions, shredded Cheddar cheese, sliced pickled jalapeño peppers and/or sour cream

1. Heat oil in large saucepan or Dutch oven over medium-high heat. Add beef, onion and garlic; cook 5 minutes, stirring occasionally. Add chili powder, cumin, salt, oregano and ground red pepper; mix well.

2. Add tomatoes, beer and salsa; bring to a boil. Reduce heat; cover and simmer 1¼ hours or until beef is very tender, stirring once.

3. Stir in beans. Simmer, uncovered, 20 minutes or until thickened as desired.

4. Ladle into bowls; serve with desired toppings.

MAKES 6 TO 8 SERVINGS

TIP

To pack this recipe for a tailgate party, cool it to room temperature at the end of step 3 and pack in a food storage container. Wrap toppings separately in small containers; keep chilled until serving. Reheat chili in covered pot on grill until hot, about 15 to 20 minutes. Serve with desired toppings.

TOMATO TEQUILA CHILI

2 pounds ground beef

2 cups finely chopped white onions

1 to 2 dried de arbol chiles

2 cloves garlic, minced

1 teaspoon ground cumin

½ to 1 teaspoon salt

¼ teaspoon ground cloves

1 can (28 ounces) whole tomatoes, coarsely chopped and juice reserved

½ cup orange juice

½ cup tequila

¼ cup tomato paste

1 tablespoon grated orange peel

Lime wedges and sprigs fresh cilantro (optional)

1. Brown beef in large skillet over medium-high heat 6 to 8 minutes, stirring to break up meat. Drain fat. Reduce heat to medium. Add onions; cook and stir 5 minutes or until tender.

2. Crush chiles into fine flakes in mortar with pestle or use spice grinder. Add chiles, garlic, cumin, salt and cloves to skillet; cook and stir 30 seconds.

3. Stir in tomatoes with juice, orange juice, tequila, tomato paste and orange peel. Bring to a boil over high heat. Reduce heat to low; cover and simmer 1½ hours, stirring occasionally.

4. Uncover skillet. Cook and stir chili over medium-low heat 10 to 15 minutes or until thickened slightly. Ladle into bowls. Serve with lime wedges and cilantro, if desired.

MAKES 6 TO 8 SERVINGS

BEST EVER CHILI

1½ pounds ground beef

1 cup chopped onion

2 cans (about 15 ounces each) kidney beans, drained with 1 cup liquid reserved

1½ pounds plum tomatoes, diced

1 can (about 15 ounces) tomato paste

¼ cup chili powder

1 teaspoon salt

Sour cream and sliced green onions (optional)

SLOW COOKER DIRECTIONS

1. Brown beef and onion in large skillet over medium-high heat 6 to 8 minutes, stirring to break up meat. Drain fat. Transfer to slow cooker.

2. Add beans, bean liquid, tomatoes, tomato paste, chili powder and salt to slow cooker; mix well. Cover; cook on LOW 10 to 12 hours.

3. Top with sour cream and green onions, if desired.

MAKES 8 SERVINGS

SIMPLE GOLDEN CORNBREAD

1¼ cups all-purpose flour

¾ cup yellow cornmeal

⅓ cup sugar

2 teaspoons baking powder

1 teaspoon salt

1¼ cups whole milk

¼ cup (½ stick) butter, melted

1 egg

Honey Butter (recipe follows, optional)

1. Preheat oven to 400°F. Spray 8-inch square baking dish or pan with nonstick cooking spray.

2. Combine flour, cornmeal, sugar, baking powder and salt in large bowl; mix well. Whisk milk, butter and egg in medium bowl until well blended. Add to flour mixture; stir just until dry ingredients are moistened. Pour batter into prepared baking dish.

3. Bake 25 minutes or until golden brown and toothpick inserted into center comes out clean.

4. Prepare Honey Butter, if desired. Serve with warm cornbread.

MAKES 9 TO 12 SERVINGS

HONEY BUTTER

Beat 6 tablespoons (¾ stick) softened butter and ¼ cup honey in medium bowl with electric mixer at medium-high speed until light and creamy.

JALAPEÑO CHEDDAR CORNBREAD

1 cup yellow cornmeal

¾ cup all-purpose flour

⅓ cup sugar

2 teaspoons baking powder

1 teaspoon salt

1 cup buttermilk or whole milk

2 eggs

3 tablespoons butter, melted

1 cup (4 ounces) shredded Cheddar cheese

2 jalapeño peppers, seeded and minced (about ⅓ cup)

1. Preheat oven to 400°F. Spray 8-inch round baking pan with nonstick cooking spray.

2. Combine cornmeal, flour, sugar, baking powder and salt in large bowl; mix well. Beat buttermilk, eggs and butter in medium bowl until blended. Add to cornmeal mixture; stir just until blended. Stir in cheese and jalapeño pepperss until blended. Spread batter evenly in prepared pan; smooth top.

3. Bake 18 to 20 minutes or until top is golden brown and toothpick inserted into center comes out clean. Cool in pan on wire rack 10 minutes; remove to serving plate. Cut into wedges to serve.

MAKES 8 SERVINGS

MEXICAN CORNBREAD PUDDING

1 can (14¾ ounces)
   cream-style corn

2 eggs

1 can (4 ounces) diced mild
   green chiles

2 tablespoons vegetable oil

¾ cup yellow cornmeal

2 tablespoons sugar

2 teaspoons baking powder

¾ teaspoon salt

½ cup (2 ounces) shredded
   Cheddar cheese

SLOW COOKER DIRECTIONS

1. Coat 2-quart slow cooker with nonstick cooking spray. Combine corn, eggs, chiles, oil, cornmeal, sugar, baking powder and salt in medium bowl; stir well to blend. Pour into slow cooker.

2. Cover; cook on LOW 2 to 2½ hours or until center is set. Sprinkle cheese over top. Cover and let stand 5 minutes or until cheese is melted.

MAKES 8 SERVINGS

SUPER SANDWICHES

BLT SUPREME

- 1 package (12 to 16 ounces) thick-cut bacon
- 1/3 cup mayonnaise
- 1 1/2 teaspoons minced chipotle pepper in adobo sauce
- 1 teaspoon lime juice
- 1 ripe avocado
- 1/8 teaspoon salt
- 1/8 teaspoon black pepper
- 4 leaves romaine lettuce
- 1/2 baguette, cut into 2 (8-inch) lengths or 2 hoagie rolls, split and toasted
- 6 to 8 slices tomato

1. Cook bacon in large skillet until crisp. Drain on paper towel-lined plate.

2. Meanwhile, combine mayonnaise, chipotle pepper and lime juice in small bowl; mix well. Coarsely mash avocado in another small bowl; stir in salt and pepper. Cut lettuce crosswise into 1/4-inch strips.

3. For each sandwich, spread heaping tablespoon mayonnaise mixture on bottom half of baguette; top with one fourth of lettuce. Arrange 3 to 4 slices bacon over lettuce; spread 2 tablespoons mashed avocado over bacon. Drizzle with heaping tablespoon mayonnaise mixture. Top with 3 to 4 tomato slices, one fourth of lettuce and 3 to 4 slices bacon. Close sandwich with top half of baguette.

MAKES 2 SERVINGS

FRENCH DIP SANDWICHES

3 pounds boneless beef chuck roast

½ teaspoon salt

½ teaspoon black pepper

1 tablespoon olive oil

2 large onions, cut into halves, then cut into ¼-inch slices

2¼ cups beef broth, divided

3 tablespoons Worcestershire sauce

6 hoagie rolls, split

12 slices provolone cheese

1. Season beef with salt and pepper. Heat oil in Dutch oven or large saucepan over medium-high heat. Add beef; cook about 6 minutes per side or until browned. Remove to plate.

2. Add onions and ¼ cup broth to Dutch oven; cook 8 minutes or until golden brown, stirring occasionally and scraping up browned bits from bottom of Dutch oven. Remove half of onions to small bowl; set aside. Stir in remaining 2 cups broth and Worcestershire sauce; mix well. Return beef to Dutch oven. Reduce heat to low; cover and cook 3 to 3½ hours or until beef is fork-tender.

3. Remove beef to large bowl; let stand until cool enough to handle. Shred into bite-size pieces. Add ⅔ cup cooking liquid; toss to coat. Pour remaining cooking liquid into small bowls for serving. Preheat broiler. Line baking sheet with foil.

4. Place rolls cut side up on prepared baking sheet; broil until lightly browned. Top bottom halves of rolls with 2 cheese slices, beef and reserved onions. Serve with warm au jus for dipping.

MAKES 6 SERVINGS

ITALIAN BEEF SANDWICHES

1 jar (16 ounces) sliced pepperoncini

1 jar (16 ounces) giardiniera

2 to 2½ pounds boneless beef chuck roast

½ cup beef broth

1 tablespoon Italian seasoning

4 French or sub rolls, split

1. Drain pepperoncini, reserving ½ cup liquid. Set aside ½ cup pepperoncini for sandwiches. Drain giardiniera, reserving ½ cup vegetables for sandwiches.

2. Combine beef, remaining pepperoncini and reserved ½ cup pepperoncini liquid, remaining giardiniera vegetables, broth and Italian seasoning in Dutch oven or large saucepan.

3. Bring to a boil over medium-high heat. Reduce heat to low; cover and cook 3 to 3½ hours or until beef is fork-tender.

4. Remove beef to large bowl; let stand until cool enough to handle. Shred beef into bite-size pieces. Add ½ cup cooking liquid; toss to coat.

5. Fill rolls with beef, reserved pepperoncini and reserved giardiniera vegetables. Serve with warm cooking liquid for dipping.

MAKES 4 SERVINGS

SPEEDY MEATBALL SUBS

1 jar (24 ounces) pasta
   sauce

1 pound frozen cooked
   Italian-style meatballs

6 sub or hoagie rolls, split

12 slices provolone cheese

   Chopped fresh parsley
   (optional)

1. Combine pasta sauce and meatballs in large saucepan. Bring to a boil over medium heat. Reduce heat to low; cover and simmer 20 minutes or until meatballs are heated through.

2. Preheat oven to 400°F. Line baking sheet with foil. Place rolls on prepared baking sheet. Bake 3 minutes or until lightly toasted.

3. Spoon sauce and meatballs on bottom halves of rolls; top with cheese slices (two per sandwich). Bake about 3 minutes or until cheese melts. Sprinkle with parsley, if desired; top with top halves of rolls.

MAKES 6 SERVINGS

TURKEY ONION DIP

Herb-Roasted Turkey
  Breast (recipe follows)
1 tablespoon olive oil
2 large onions, cut in half
  crosswise then cut into
  ¼-inch slices (about
  2 cups)
¼ cup water
½ teaspoon salt, plus
  additional for seasoning
1½ cups sour cream
⅓ cup prepared horseradish
3 tablespoons Dijon mustard
  Black pepper
6 hoagie or sub rolls, split
  and toasted
12 slices Swiss cheese (about
  1 ounce each)

1. Prepare Herb-Roasted Turkey Breast.

2. Meanwhile, heat oil in large skillet over medium-high heat. Add onions; cook 20 minutes or until onions begin to brown, stirring occasionally. Add water and ½ teaspoon salt; cook over medium heat 20 minutes or until golden brown, stirring occasionally.

3. Combine sour cream, horseradish and mustard in medium bowl; stir until well blended. Refrigerate until ready to assemble sandwiches.

4. Shred turkey into bite-size pieces; place in large bowl. Drizzle with pan juices and season with additional salt and pepper; toss to coat.

5. Spread cut sides of each roll with about 1½ tablespoons sour cream mixture. Top bottom halves of rolls with 2 cups turkey, caramelized onions, 2 slices cheese and top halves of rolls. Serve warm.

MAKES 6 SERVINGS

HERB-ROASTED TURKEY BREAST

1 small bone-in turkey
  breast (4 to 5 pounds)
1½ tablespoons olive oil
2 cloves garlic, minced
2 teaspoons coarse salt
1 teaspoon dried rosemary
1 teaspoon dried sage
½ teaspoon dried thyme
½ teaspoon black pepper

1. Preheat oven to 400°F. Place turkey breast on rack in small roasting or baking pan. Pat skin dry with paper towel.

2. Combine oil, garlic, salt, rosemary, sage, thyme and pepper in small bowl; mix well. Rub mixture all over turkey breast. (If desired, loosen skin and rub some of oil mixture directly on turkey meat.)

3. Place turkey in oven; *reduce oven temperature to 350°F.* Roast 1 hour and 15 minutes or until cooked through (165°F). Let rest 15 minutes.

MAKES ABOUT 6 SERVINGS

BARBECUE BEEF SANDWICHES

2½ pounds boneless beef chuck roast

2 tablespoons Southwest seasoning

1 tablespoon vegetable oil

1¼ cups beef broth

2½ cups barbecue sauce, divided

1⅓ cups prepared coleslaw* (preferably vinegar based)

4 sandwich rolls or pretzel buns, split

Prepared coleslaw can be found in the deli department at most supermarkets. Vinegar-based coleslaws provide a perfect complement to the rich beef but mayonnaise-based slaw will also work.

1. Sprinkle both sides of beef with Southwest seasoning. Heat oil in Dutch oven over medium-high heat. Add beef; cook about 6 minutes per side or until browned. Remove to plate.

2. Add broth; cook 2 minutes, scraping up browned bits from bottom of Dutch oven. Stir in 2 cups barbecue sauce; bring to a boil. Return beef to Dutch oven; turn to coat.

3. Reduce heat to low; cover and cook 3 to 3½ hours or until beef is fork-tender, turning beef halfway through cooking time.

4. Remove beef to large plate; let stand until cool enough to handle. Meanwhile, cook sauce remaining in Dutch oven over high heat about 10 minutes or until reduced and slightly thickened.

5. Shred beef into bite-size pieces. Stir in 1 cup reduced cooking sauce and ¼ cup barbecue sauce. Add remaining ¼ cup barbecue sauce, if desired. Serve beef and coleslaw on rolls.

MAKES 4 SERVINGS

THE GREAT REUBEN SANDWICH

¼ cup Thousand Island
  dressing (see Tip)

4 slices rye bread

8 ounces thinly sliced
  corned beef or pastrami

4 slices Swiss cheese

½ cup sauerkraut, well
  drained

2 tablespoons butter

1. Spread dressing on one side of each bread slice. Top two bread slices with corned beef, cheese, sauerkraut and remaining bread slices.

2. Melt butter in large skillet over medium heat. Add sandwiches; press down with spatula or weigh down with small plate. Cook sandwiches 6 minutes per side or until cheese is melted and bread is lightly browned, pressing down with spatula to crisp bread slightly. Serve immediately.

MAKES 2 SANDWICHES

TIP

Purchase bottled Thousand Island dressing or make your own. Combine 2 tablespoons mayonnaise, 2 tablespoons sweet pickle relish and 1 tablespoon cocktail sauce in small bowl.

SLOW COOKER GREEN CHILE PULLED PORK SANDWICHES

3½ to 4 pounds bone-in or boneless pork shoulder

1 teaspoon salt

½ teaspoon black pepper

1 can (about 14 ounces) diced tomatoes with green chiles

1 cup chopped onion

½ cup water

2 tablespoons fresh lime juice

1 teaspoon ground cumin

1 teaspoon minced garlic

2 whole canned chipotle peppers in adobo sauce, minced

8 hard rolls or hoagie buns

½ cup sour cream (optional)

2 ripe avocados, sliced

3 tablespoons chopped fresh cilantro (optional)

SLOW COOKER DIRECTIONS

1. Season pork with salt and black pepper and place in slow cooker.

2. Combine tomatoes, onion, water, lime juice, cumin, garlic and chipotle peppers in medium bowl. Pour over pork.

3. Cover and cook on LOW 7 to 8 hours or until pork shreds easily when tested with fork.

4. Remove pork to cutting board and cool slightly. Remove any fat from surface of meat and discard. Shred pork with two forks. Return pork to cooking liquid; stir to combine.

5. Serve pork on rolls with sour cream, avocado slices and cilantro, if desired.

MAKES 8 SERVINGS

HOISIN BARBECUE CHICKEN SLIDERS

⅔ cup hoisin sauce

⅓ cup barbecue sauce

3 tablespoons quick-cooking tapioca

1 tablespoon sugar

1 tablespoon soy sauce

¼ teaspoon red pepper flakes

12 boneless skinless chicken thighs (3 to 3½ pounds total)

16 dinner rolls or Hawaiian sweet rolls, split

½ medium red onion, finely chopped

Sliced pickles (optional)

SLOW COOKER DIRECTIONS

1. Combine hoisin sauce, barbecue sauce, tapioca, sugar, soy sauce and red pepper flakes in slow cooker; mix well. Add chicken. Cover; cook on LOW 8 to 9 hours.

2. Remove chicken from sauce. Coarsely shred with two forks. Return shredded chicken to slow cooker; mix well.

3. Spoon ¼ cup chicken and sauce on each bun. Serve with onion and pickles, if desired.

MAKES 16 SLIDERS

CHICKEN MEATBALL GRINDERS

1 pound ground chicken

½ cup fresh whole wheat or white bread crumbs (1 slice bread)

1 egg white, lightly beaten

3 tablespoons finely chopped fresh parsley

2 cloves garlic, minced

½ teaspoon salt

⅛ teaspoon black pepper

1 tablespoon olive oil

½ cup chopped onion

1 can (about 14 ounces) diced tomatoes

1 can (8 ounces) tomato sauce

2 tablespoons tomato paste

1 teaspoon Italian seasoning

4 small hard rolls, split

2 tablespoons grated Parmesan cheese

1. Combine chicken, bread crumbs, egg white, parsley, garlic, ½ teaspoon salt and ⅛ teaspoon pepper in medium bowl. Shape mixture into 12 to 16 meatballs.

2. Heat oil in medium nonstick skillet over medium heat. Add meatballs; cook about 5 minutes or until browned on all sides, turning occasionally. Remove meatballs from skillet.

3. Add onion to skillet; cook and stir 3 minutes. Stir in tomatoes, tomato sauce, tomato paste and Italian seasoning; bring to a boil. Reduce heat to low and simmer, covered, 15 minutes. Season with salt and pepper. Return meatballs to skillet; simmer, covered, 15 minutes.

4. Place 3 to 4 meatballs in each roll. Spoon sauce evenly over meatballs. Sprinkle with cheese.

MAKES 4 SERVINGS

SLOPPY JOES

- 3 pounds ground beef
- 1 cup chopped onion
- 1 cup chopped red bell pepper
- 3 cloves garlic, minced
- 1¼ cups ketchup
- ¼ cup plus 1 tablespoon Worcestershire sauce
- ¼ cup packed brown sugar
- 3 tablespoons prepared mustard
- 3 tablespoons cider vinegar
- 2 teaspoons chili powder
- Toasted hamburger buns

1. Brown beef, onion, bell pepper and garlic in large skillet over medium-high heat 6 to 8 minutes, stirring to break up meat.

2. Stir in ketchup, Worcestershire sauce, brown sugar, mustard, vinegar and chili powder; bring to a boil over high heat. Reduce heat; simmer 20 minutes or until mixture has thickened. Serve on buns.

MAKES 8 SERVINGS

PASTRAMI SANDWICHES WITH MUSTARD

1½ cups beef broth

1 cup dark beer

1 teaspoon Worcestershire sauce

1 pound thinly sliced pastrami

6 French sandwich rolls

12 slices Swiss cheese

Dijon mustard

1. Combine broth, beer and Worcestershire sauce in medium saucepan. Bring to boil. Reduce heat to low. Separate layers of pastrami and add to saucepan. Cook until pastrami is heated through.

2. Preheat broiler. Split sandwich rolls and place on baking sheet. Place pastrami on bottom half of each roll; reserve cooking liquid. Top each roll with 2 cheese slices. Broil 1 to 2 minutes or until cheese is melted and bubbly. Spread mustard over top halves of rolls; close sandwiches. Serve sandwiches with reserved cooking liquid for dipping.

MAKES 6 SERVINGS

HONEY-MUSTARD AND BEER PULLED PORK SANDWICHES

1 tablespoon chili powder

2 teaspoons ground cumin

1 teaspoon salt

¼ teaspoon black pepper

2 tablespoons yellow mustard

2½ to 3 pounds bone-in pork shoulder roast

2 bottles (12 ounces each) beer, divided

¾ cup ketchup

3 tablespoons honey

2 tablespoons cider vinegar

8 soft sandwich rolls

24 bread and butter pickle chips

1. Prepare grill for indirect cooking over medium-low heat.

2. Combine chili powder, cumin, salt and pepper in small bowl. Spread mustard on all sides of pork; pat spice mixture all over pork. Transfer pork to rack in disposable foil pan. Reserve ¾ cup beer. Pour enough remaining beer into foil pan to just cover rack beneath pork. Place tray on grid opposite heat source. Grill, covered, 4 to 6 hours or until internal temperature reaches 160°F. Remove to cutting board, tent with foil and let stand 15 minutes.

3. Combine reserved ¾ cup beer, ketchup, honey and vinegar in small saucepan. Bring to a boil over medium-high heat. Reduce heat to medium; cook until thickened, stirring occasionally.

4. Shred pork with two forks, discarding any bone, fat or connective tissue. Combine pork and sauce in medium bowl; toss gently to combine. Serve on rolls with pickles.

MAKES 8 SERVINGS

ULTIMATE BURGERS

CLASSIC GRILLED BURGERS

1½ pounds ground beef

1½ teaspoons kosher salt *or* 1¼ teaspoons regular salt

½ teaspoon black pepper

4 hamburger buns, split

Sliced tomatoes, lettuce leaves, sliced red onion and pickle slices

Condiments: ketchup, mayonnaise and/or mustard

1. Shape beef into four patties. Combine salt and pepper in small bowl; sprinkle over both sides of patties. Make 1-inch wide shallow indentation in center of each patty to discourage shrinkage.

2. Prepare grill for direct cooking. Oil grid.

3. Place patties on grid over medium-high heat. Grill, covered, 2½ minutes or until browned on bottom. Turn and grill until other sides are browned and meat still feels soft when pressed in center with finger, about 2½ minutes more for medium-rare. If flare-ups occur, move to outer edge of charcoal grill (not over coals) or a turned-off area of gas grill. Transfer to plate. Place buns on grid, cut sides down; grill until toasted, about 1 minute.

4. Serve burgers on buns with desired toppings and condiments.

MAKES 4 SERVINGS

THE ROYAL BURGER

1 teaspoon Royal Seasoning (recipe follows), divided

4 slices bacon

12 ounces ground beef

2 slices deli American cheese

2 eggs
   Salt and black pepper

2 sesame seed buns, split and toasted

2 tablespoons mayonnaise

½ cup shredded lettuce

4 slices ripe tomato

1. Prepare Royal Seasoning.

2. Cook bacon in large skillet until crisp. Drain on paper towel-lined plate. Pour off all but 1 teaspoon drippings from skillet. (Reserve some of bacon drippings for frying eggs, if desired.)

3. Combine beef and ¾ teaspoon Royal Seasoning in medium bowl; mix gently. Shape into two 5-inch patties. Sprinkle both sides of patties with remaining ¼ teaspoon seasoning mix.

4. Return skillet to medium heat. Cook patties about 5 minutes per side or until cooked through (160°F).* Top each burger with cheese slice during last minute of cooking.

5. While burgers are cooking, heat 2 teaspoons reserved bacon drippings or butter in another large skillet or griddle over medium heat. Crack eggs into skillet; cook 3 to 4 minutes or until whites are set and yolks begin to thicken and firm around edges. Season with salt and pepper.

6. Spread cut sides of buns with mayonnaise. Top bottom buns with lettuce, burgers, bacon, tomato, eggs and tops of buns.

Patties can also be grilled or broiled 5 minutes per side or until cooked through.

MAKES 2 SERVINGS

ROYAL SEASONING

- 2 tablespoons salt
- 1½ tablespoons paprika
- 1 tablespoon garlic powder
- ½ tablespoon onion powder
- ½ tablespoon chili powder
- ¾ teaspoon ground cumin
- ¾ teaspoon dried basil
- ¾ teaspoon black pepper
- ¼ teaspoon dried oregano

Combine all ingredients in small bowl; mix well. Store in airtight container. Seasoning mix can be used for steaks, chicken and vegetables in addition to burgers.

MAKES ABOUT ¹/₃ CUP

DELUXE MEDITERRANEAN LAMB BURGERS

1½ pounds ground lamb

1 tablespoon minced garlic

2 teaspoons Greek seasoning

1 teaspoon paprika

½ teaspoon salt, divided

½ teaspoon black pepper

4 thin slices red onion, separated into rings

1 tablespoon olive oil

1 teaspoon chopped fresh mint or parsley

1 teaspoon red wine vinegar

   Spinach leaves

4 whole grain rolls, split and toasted

4 to 8 slices tomatoes

1 package (4 ounces) feta cheese crumbles

1. Prepare grill for direct cooking.

2. Combine lamb, garlic, Greek seasoning, paprika, ¼ teaspoon salt and pepper in large bowl; mix gently but thoroughly. Shape into four patties about ¾ inch thick.

3. Combine onion, oil, mint, vinegar and remaining ¼ teaspoon salt in small bowl; toss to coat.

4. Place patties on grid. Grill, covered, over medium heat 8 to 10 minutes (or uncovered, 13 to 15 minutes) to medium (160°F) or to desired doneness, turning once.

5. Place spinach on bottom halves of rolls. Top with burgers, tomatoes, onion mixture and feta cheese. Cover with top halves of rolls.

MAKES 4 SERVINGS

CURRIED BEEF BURGERS

1 **pound ground beef**

¼ **cup mango chutney, chopped**

¼ **cup grated apple**

1½ **teaspoons curry powder**

½ **teaspoon salt**

⅛ **teaspoon black pepper**

1 **large red onion, cut into ¼-inch slices**

Lettuce leaves

4 **Kaiser rolls or hamburger buns**

1 **large tomato, sliced**

1. Prepare grill for direct cooking.

2. Combine beef, chutney, apple, curry powder, salt and pepper in medium bowl; mix gently but thoroughly. Shape into four patties.

3. Place patties on grid. Grill, covered, over medium heat 8 to 10 minutes (or uncovered, 13 to 15 minutes) or until cooked through (160°F), turning once.

4. Grill onion 5 minutes or until lightly charred, turning once. Place lettuce on bottom halves of rolls. Top with burgers, tomato, onion and tops of rolls.

MAKES 4 SERVINGS

CUBANO BURGERS

1½ pounds ground pork

¼ cup minced green onions

3 tablespoons yellow mustard, divided

1 tablespoon minced garlic

2 teaspoons paprika

½ teaspoon black pepper

¼ teaspoon salt

8 slices Swiss cheese

4 bolillos or Kaiser rolls, split and toasted

8 slices sandwich-style dill pickles

¼ pound thinly sliced ham

1. Prepare grill for direct cooking.

2. Combine pork, green onions, 1 tablespoon mustard, garlic, paprika, pepper and salt in large bowl; mix gently but thoroughly. Shape into four patties about ¾ inch thick, shaping to fit rolls.

3. Place patties on grid. Grill, covered, over medium heat 8 to 10 minutes (or uncovered, 13 to 15 minutes) or until cooked through (160°F), turning occasionally. Top each burger with 2 cheese slices during last 2 minutes of grilling.

4. Spread remaining 2 tablespoons mustard over cut sides of rolls. Place pickles on bottom half of each roll. Top each with burger and ham. Cover with top halves of rolls. Press down firmly.

MAKES 4 SERVINGS

SUBSTITUTION

A bolillo is an oval-shaped roll about 6 inches long with a crunchy crust and a soft inside. If you can't find bolillos, use a loaf of French bread. Cut in half and then into individual-sized portions.

BRIE BURGERS WITH SUN-DRIED TOMATO AND ARTICHOKE SPREAD

- 1 cup canned quartered artichokes, drained and chopped
- ½ cup oil-packed sun-dried tomatoes, drained and chopped, divided
- 2 tablespoons mayonnaise
- 1 tablespoon plus 1 teaspoon minced garlic, divided
- 1 teaspoon black pepper, divided
- ½ teaspoon salt, divided
- 1½ pounds ground beef
- ¼ cup chopped shallots
- ¼ pound Brie cheese, sliced
- 2 tablespoons butter, softened
- 4 egg or Kaiser rolls, split
  Heirloom tomato slices
  Arugula or lettuce leaves

1. Prepare grill for direct cooking.

2. Combine artichokes, ¼ cup sun-dried tomatoes, mayonnaise, 1 teaspoon garlic, ½ teaspoon pepper and ¼ teaspoon salt in small bowl; mix well.

3. Combine beef, shallots, remaining ¼ cup sun-dried tomatoes, 1 tablespoon garlic, ½ teaspoon pepper and ¼ teaspoon salt in large bowl; mix gently but thoroughly. Shape into four patties.

4. Place patties on grid. Grill, covered, over medium heat 8 to 10 minutes (or uncovered, 13 to 15 minutes) or until cooked through (160°F), turning occasionally. Top each burger with cheese during last 2 minutes of grilling.

5. Spread butter on cut surfaces of rolls; grill or toast until lightly browned. Spread artichoke mixture on bottoms of rolls. Top with tomato slice, burger and arugula. Cover with tops of rolls.

MAKES 4 SERVINGS

BACON SMASHBURGER

4 slices bacon, cut in half

1 pound ground beef
   Salt and black pepper

4 slices sharp Cheddar
   cheese

4 eggs (optional)

4 brioche rolls or hamburger
   buns

1. Cook bacon in large skillet over medium-high heat until crisp. Drain on paper towel-lined plate. Drain all but 1 tablespoon drippings from skillet.

2. Divide beef into four portions and shape lightly into loose balls. Place in same skillet over medium-high heat. Smash with spatula to flatten into thin patties; sprinkle with salt and pepper. Cook 2 to 3 minutes or until edges and bottoms are browned. Flip burgers and top with cheese. Cook 2 to 3 minutes for medium-rare or to desired doneness. Transfer to plates.

3. If desired, crack eggs into hot skillet. Cook over medium heat about 3 minutes or until whites are opaque and yolks are desired degree of doneness, flipping once, if desired, for overeasy. Place burgers on rolls; top with eggs and bacon.

MAKES 4 SERVINGS

GREAT GRILLING

BOLD AND ZESTY BEEF BACK RIBS

5 pounds beef back ribs, cut into 3- or 4-rib portions

Salt and black pepper

1 teaspoon vegetable oil

1 small onion, minced

2 cloves garlic, minced

1 cup ketchup

½ cup chili sauce

2 tablespoons lemon juice

1 tablespoon packed brown sugar

1 teaspoon hot pepper sauce

1. Place ribs in shallow pan; season with salt and black pepper. Refrigerate until ready to grill.

2. For sauce, heat oil in medium saucepan over medium heat. Add onion and garlic; cook and stir 5 minutes or until onion is tender. Stir in ketchup, chili sauce, lemon juice, brown sugar and hot pepper sauce. Reduce heat to medium-low. Cook 15 minutes, stirring occasionally.

3. Meanwhile, prepare grill for indirect cooking.

4. Place ribs on grid directly over drip pan. Baste ribs generously with some of sauce. Grill, covered, 45 to 60 minutes or until ribs are tender and browned, turning occasionally.

5. Bring remaining sauce to a boil over medium-high heat; boil 1 minute. Serve ribs with sauce.

MAKES 5 TO 6 SERVINGS

SPICY BARBECUED CHICKEN

1 tablespoon paprika or smoked paprika

1 teaspoon dried thyme

½ teaspoon salt

½ teaspoon dried sage

¼ teaspoon black pepper

¼ teaspoon ground red pepper

1 whole chicken (3½ to 4 pounds), quartered

¾ cup ketchup

½ cup packed brown sugar

2 tablespoons soy sauce

2 tablespoons Worcestershire sauce

1 clove garlic, minced

1. Combine paprika, thyme, salt, sage, black pepper and red pepper in small bowl. Press mixture all over chicken. Transfer chicken to large resealable food storage bag. Seal bag; refrigerate up to 24 hours.

2. For basting sauce, mix ketchup, brown sugar, soy sauce, Worcestershire sauce and garlic in small bowl.

3. Prepare grill for direct cooking. Place chicken on grid over medium to medium-low heat. Grill chicken, covered, over medium heat 30 to 40 minutes, turning occasionally or until cooked through (165°F). Brush chicken generously with some of basting sauce during last 10 minutes of cooking. Serve with remaining sauce.

MAKES 4 SERVINGS

CEDAR PLANK SALMON WITH GRILLED CITRUS MANGO

4 salmon fillets (6 ounces each), skin intact

2 teaspoons sugar, divided

1 teaspoon chili powder

½ teaspoon black pepper

¼ teaspoon salt

¼ teaspoon ground allspice

¼ cup chopped fresh mint

2 tablespoons orange juice

1 tablespoon lemon juice

1 tablespoon lime juice

2 teaspoons minced fresh ginger

⅛ teaspoon red pepper flakes

2 medium mangoes, peeled and cut into 1-inch pieces

1 cedar plank (about 15×7 inches, ½ inch thick), soaked*

*Soak in water 5 hours or overnight.

1. Prepare grill for direct cooking over medium-high heat.

2. Rinse and pat dry salmon fillets. Combine 1 teaspoon sugar, chili powder, black pepper, salt and allspice in small bowl. Rub evenly over flesh side of fillets.

3. Combine remaining 1 teaspoon sugar, mint, orange, lemon and lime juices, ginger and red pepper flakes in medium bowl; mix well.

4. Thread mango pieces onto skewers or spread out in grill basket.

5. If using charcoal grill, wait until coals are covered with gray ash to start grilling salmon. If using gas grill, turn heat down to medium. Keep clean spray bottle filled with water nearby in case plank begins to burn. If it flares up, spray lightly with water.

6. Lightly brush grid with oil and place soaked plank on top. Cover and heat until plank smokes and crackles. Place salmon, skin side down, on plank and arrange mango skewers alongside plank. Grill, covered, 6 to 8 minutes, turning skewers frequently, until mango pieces are slightly charred. Remove mango from the grill; set aside. Cover; grill salmon 9 to 12 minutes or until the flesh begins to flake when tested with fork.

7. Remove plank from grill and transfer salmon to serving platter. Slide mango pieces off skewers and add to mint mixture, tossing gently to coat. Serve immediately with salmon.

MAKES 4 SERVINGS

GRILLED VIETNAMESE-STYLE CHICKEN WINGS

3 pounds chicken wings

⅓ cup honey

¼ to ½ cup sliced lemongrass

¼ cup fish sauce

2 tablespoons chopped garlic

2 tablespoons chopped shallots

2 tablespoons chopped fresh ginger

2 tablespoons lime juice

2 tablespoons canola oil

Chopped fresh cilantro (optional)

1. Remove and discard wing tips. Cut each wing in half at joint. Place wings in large resealable food storage bag.

2. Combine honey, lemongrass, fish sauce, garlic, shallots, ginger, lime juice and oil in food processor; process until smooth. Pour over wings. Seal bag; turn to coat. Marinate in refrigerator 4 hours or overnight.

3. Prepare grill for direct cooking over medium heat.

4. Remove wings from marinade; reserve marinade. Grill wings 35 to 45 minutes or until cooked through, browned and crispy, turning and basting occasionally with marinade (do not baste during last 5 minutes of grilling); discard any remaining marinade. Garnish with cilantro.

MAKES 6 TO 8 SERVINGS

BEER-BASTED BARBECUE PORK CHOPS

1 cup barbecue sauce, divided

1 cup plus 3 tablespoons beer, divided

3 tablespoons honey

1 tablespoon chili powder

6 bone-in loin pork chops, about 1 inch thick

1 teaspoon salt

½ teaspoon black pepper

1. Combine ½ cup barbecue sauce, 1 cup beer, honey and chili powder in large bowl. Add pork chops; turn to coat. Refrigerate 2 to 4 hours, turning occasionally. Combine remaining ½ cup barbecue sauce and 3 tablespoons beer in separate bowl; set aside.

2. Prepare grill for direct cooking over medium-high heat. Oil grid.

3. Remove pork from marinade; sprinkle with salt and pepper.

4. Place pork on grid. Grill over medium-high heat 4 minutes. Turn chops over; brush with half of reserved barbecue sauce mixture. Grill 3 minutes. Turn over; brush with remaining sauce mixture and grill 4 to 5 minutes or until an instant read thermometer inserted into the thickest portion of pork registers 150°F.

MAKES 6 SERVINGS

MAPLE FRANCHEEZIES

- ½ cup yellow mustard
- 1 tablespoon finely chopped onion
- 1 tablespoon diced tomato
- 1 tablespoon chopped fresh parsley
- 3 teaspoons garlic powder, divided
- 1½ teaspoons black pepper, divided
- ¼ cup maple syrup
- ½ teaspoon ground nutmeg
- 4 slices bacon
- 4 jumbo hot dogs
- 4 hot dog buns, split
- ½ cup (2 ounces) shredded Cheddar cheese

1. Combine mustard, onion, tomato, parsley, 1 teaspoon garlic powder and ½ teaspoon pepper in small bowl; set aside.

2. Prepare grill for direct cooking.

3. Combine maple syrup, remaining 2 teaspoons garlic powder, remaining 1 teaspoon pepper and nutmeg in small bowl. Brush syrup mixture onto bacon slices. Wrap 1 bacon slice around each hot dog.

4. Brush hot dogs with remaining syrup mixture. Grill hot dogs, covered, over medium-high heat 8 minutes or until bacon is crisp and hot dogs are heated through, turning once. Place hot dogs in buns; top with sauce mixture and cheese.

MAKES 4 SERVINGS

HONEY-MUSTARD GLAZED CHICKEN

1 whole chicken
  (4 to 5 pounds)

1 tablespoon vegetable oil

¼ cup honey

2 tablespoons Dijon
  mustard

1 tablespoon soy sauce

½ teaspoon ground ginger

⅛ teaspoon black pepper

  Dash salt

1. Prepare grill for indirect cooking.

2. Remove giblets from chicken cavity and discard. Pull chicken skin over neck; secure with metal skewer. Tuck wings under back; tie legs together with wet string. Lightly brush chicken with oil.

3. Combine honey, mustard, soy sauce, ginger, pepper and salt in small bowl; set aside.

4. Place chicken, breast side up, on grid directly over drip pan. Grill, covered, over medium-high heat 1 hour 30 minutes or until cooked through (165°F) for both light and dark meat. Brush with glaze every 10 minutes during last 30 minutes of cooking time.*

5. Remove chicken to cutting board; tent with foil. Let stand 15 minutes before carving. Internal temperature will continue to rise 5° to 10°F during stand time.

If using grill with heat on one side (rather than around drip pan), rotate chicken 180 degrees after 45 minutes of cooking.

MAKES 4 TO 5 SERVINGS

GRILLED PORK CHOPS WITH LAGER BARBECUE SAUCE

- 1 cup lager
- ⅓ cup maple syrup
- 3 tablespoons molasses
- 1 teaspoon Mexican-style hot chili powder
- 4 bone-in center-cut pork chops, 1 inch thick (2 to 2¼ pounds)

    Lager Barbecue Sauce (recipe follows)
- ¾ teaspoon salt
- ¼ teaspoon black pepper

1. Combine beer, maple syrup, molasses, chili powder and pork chops in large resealable food storage bag. Marinate in refrigerator 2 hours, turning occasionally.

2. Meanwhile, prepare Lager Barbecue Sauce.

3. Prepare grill for direct cooking over medium-high heat. Oil grid.

4. Remove pork chops from marinade; discard marinade. Sprinkle with salt and pepper. Grill 6 to 7 minutes per side or until 150°F. Serve with Lager Barbecue Sauce.

MAKES 4 SERVINGS

LAGER BARBECUE SAUCE

- ½ cup lager
- ⅓ cup ketchup
- 3 tablespoons maple syrup
- 2 tablespoons finely chopped onion
- 1 tablespoon molasses
- 1 tablespoon cider vinegar
- ½ teaspoon Mexican-style hot chili powder

Combine beer, ketchup, maple syrup, onion, molasses, vinegar and chili powder in small saucepan. Bring to a simmer over medium heat. Cook 10 minutes or until slightly thickened, stirring occasionally.

MAKES ABOUT ½ CUP

GRILLED SWORDFISH WITH HOT RED SAUCE

2 tablespoons Sesame Salt (recipe follows)

4 swordfish or halibut steaks (about 1½ pounds total)

¼ cup chopped green onions

2 tablespoons hot bean paste*

2 tablespoons soy sauce

4 teaspoons sugar

4 cloves garlic, minced

1 tablespoon dark sesame oil

⅛ teaspoon black pepper

Available in specialty stores or Asian markets.

1. Prepare Sesame Salt.

2. Rinse swordfish and pat dry with paper towels. Place in shallow glass dish.

3. Combine green onions, 2 tablespoons Sesame Salt, hot bean paste, soy sauce, sugar, garlic, sesame oil and pepper in small bowl; mix well.

4. Spread mixture over both sides of fish; cover with plastic wrap. Marinate in refrigerator 30 minutes.

5. Prepare grill for direct cooking.

6. Remove fish from marinade; discard marinade. Grill fish over medium-high heat 4 to 5 minutes per side or until fish is opaque.

MAKES 4 SERVINGS

SESAME SALT

Heat small skillet over medium heat. Add ¼ cup sesame seeds; cook and stir about 3 minutes or until seeds are golden. Cool. Crush toasted sesame seeds and 1 teaspoon coarse salt with mortar and pestle or process in clean spice grinder. Store in airtight container in refrigerator.

SPICY SMOKED BEEF RIBS

4 wood pieces for smoking

4 to 6 pounds beef back ribs, cut into 3- to 4-rib portions

Black pepper

1⅓ cups barbecue sauce

2 teaspoons hot pepper sauce or Szechuan chili sauce

Beer, at room temperature, or hot water

1. Soak wood pieces in water at least 30 minutes; drain.

2. Spread ribs on large baking sheet; season with black pepper. Combine barbecue sauce and hot pepper sauce in small bowl. Brush ribs with half of sauce. Marinate in refrigerator 30 minutes to 1 hour.

3. Prepare grill for indirect cooking over low heat. Add soaked wood to fire. Place foil drip pan in center of grill. Fill pan half full with beer.

4. Place ribs on grid, meaty side up, directly above drip pan. Grill ribs, covered, about 1 hour or until meat is tender, brushing remaining sauce over ribs 2 or 3 times during cooking. (If grill has thermometer, maintain cooking temperature at 250° to 275°F. Add a few more briquets as needed to maintain constant temperature.) Add more soaked wood after 30 minutes, if necessary.

MAKES 4 TO 6 SERVINGS

TANGY MAPLE SYRUP BBQ DRUMS

8 chicken drumsticks, skin removed

Salt and black pepper

¼ cup maple syrup

2 tablespoons mustard

2 tablespoons soy sauce

½ teaspoon ground allspice

¼ teaspoon salt

¼ teaspoon red pepper flakes

1. Prepare grill for direct cooking. Oil grid. Spray grill rack with nonstick cooking spray and place on grid until heated.

2. Season chicken with salt and black pepper. Place chicken on grill rack. Grill, covered, over medium heat 30 minutes or until chicken is cooked through and browned, turning frequently.

3. Combine maple syrup, mustard, soy sauce, allspice, ¼ teaspoon salt and red pepper flakes in medium bowl; mix well.

4. Place grilled chicken in 13×9-inch baking pan; drizzle with sauce and turn to coat. Let stand 5 minutes, turning once.

MAKES 8 SERVINGS

APRICOT AND HONEY GLAZED BABY BACK RIBS

1 tablespoon garlic powder

1 tablespoon ground cumin

1 teaspoon salt

½ teaspoon black pepper

6 pounds pork baby back ribs (2 racks), cut in half

1 bottle (12 ounces) honey wheat lager

1 cup apricot preserves

3 tablespoons honey

1. Prepare grill for indirect cooking over medium heat. Oil grid. Combine garlic powder, cumin, salt and pepper in small bowl. Rub over both sides of ribs.

2. Grill ribs, meat side down, over medium heat 30 minutes. Turn and grill 30 minutes.

3. Meanwhile, combine beer, preserves and honey in medium saucepan over medium-high heat. Bring to a boil; cook 20 minutes or until thick and reduced to ¾ cup.

4. Turn and brush ribs with half of glaze; grill 15 minutes. Turn and brush with remaining glaze; grill 15 minutes or until ribs are tender.

MAKES 6 TO 8 SERVINGS

SERIOUSLY SWEET

CHOCOLATE-COVERED BACON

12 slices thick-cut bacon

1 cup semisweet chocolate chips

2 tablespoons shortening, divided

1 cup white chocolate chips or butterscotch chips

1. Preheat oven to 400°F. Thread each bacon slice onto 12-inch wooden skewer. Place on rack in large baking pan. Bake 20 to 25 minutes or until crisp. Cool completely.

2. Combine semisweet chocolate chips and 1 tablespoon shortening in large microwavable bowl. Microwave on HIGH at 30-second intervals until melted and smooth.

3. Combine white chocolate chips and remaining 1 tablespoon shortening in large microwavable bowl. Microwave on HIGH at 30-second intervals until melted and smooth.

4. Drizzle chocolates over each bacon slice. Place on waxed paper-lined baking sheets. Refrigerate until firm. Store in refrigerator.

MAKES 12 SLICES

HOT BROWNIE SUNDAE

¾ cup (1½ sticks) butter

4 ounces unsweetened chocolate, chopped

1¾ cups sugar

4 eggs

1 teaspoon vanilla

¾ cup all-purpose flour

½ teaspoon salt

Hot fudge sauce

Caramel ice cream topping

Vanilla ice cream

½ cup chopped pecans

1. Preheat oven to 350°F. Line 8- or 9-inch square baking pan with parchment paper or spray with nonstick cooking spray.

2. Combine butter and chocolate in medium saucepan; heat over low heat until melted, stirring frequently. Remove from heat; stir in sugar until well blended. Add eggs, one at a time, beating until well blended after each addition. Stir in vanilla. Add flour and salt; stir just until blended. Pour batter into prepared pan.

3. Bake 20 to 23 minutes or until toothpick inserted into center comes out with fudgy crumbs. Cool in pan on wire rack 10 minutes.

4. Heat hot fudge sauce and caramel topping according to package directions. Cut brownie into nine squares. For each serving, place one warm brownie on serving plate; drizzle with hot fudge sauce. Top with ice cream, caramel topping and pecans. Serve immediately.

MAKES 9 SERVINGS

CHOCOLATE CHIP
ICE CREAM SANDWICHES

1 cup biscuit baking mix

⅔ cup milk

1 egg

1 tablespoon vegetable oil

⅔ cup mini semisweet
 chocolate chips

2 cups ice cream

 Assorted sprinkles, mini
 semisweet chocolate
 chips (optional)

1. Preheat waffle maker to medium. Combine baking mix, milk, egg and oil in medium bowl. Stir in ⅔ cup chocolate chips.

2. Pour half of batter onto waffle maker; cook until golden brown and crisp. Repeat with remaining batter. Cool waffles completely.

3. Cut waffles into four segments each. Top with ½ cup ice cream and another waffle to make sandwich. Roll sides in sprinkles or chocolate chips, if desired. Wrap in foil and freeze 1 hour or until firm.

MAKES 4 SERVINGS

CHOCOLATE PEANUT BUTTER PIE

10 whole chocolate graham crackers, broken into pieces

2 tablespoons granulated sugar

¼ cup (½ stick) butter, melted

1 package (8 ounces) cream cheese, softened

1 cup creamy peanut butter

1¾ cups powdered sugar, divided

3 tablespoons butter, softened

1¾ teaspoons vanilla, divided

¼ teaspoon salt

2 cups cold whipping cream

½ cup unsweetened cocoa powder

2 packages (1½ ounces each) chocolate peanut butter cups, chopped

1. Preheat oven to 350°F. Combine graham crackers and granulated sugar in food processor; process until finely ground. Add ¼ cup melted butter; process until well blended. Press onto bottom and up side of 9-inch pie plate.

2. Bake 8 minutes. Cool completely on wire rack.

3. For filing, beat cream cheese, peanut butter, ¾ cup powdered sugar, 3 tablespoons softened butter, 1 teaspoon vanilla and salt in large bowl with electric mixer at medium speed about 3 minutes or until light and fluffy. Spread filling in cooled crust; smooth top. Place in refrigerator.

4. For topping, beat cream, remaining 1 cup powdered sugar, ¾ teaspoon vanilla and cocoa in large bowl with electric mixer at high speed 1 to 2 minutes or until soft peaks form. Spread chocolate whipped cream over peanut butter layer; sprinkle with peanut butter cups. Refrigerate several hours or overnight.

MAKES 8 SERVINGS

ICE CREAM PIZZA TREAT

24 chocolate sandwich
   cookies

 1 jar (about 12 ounces)
   hot fudge ice cream
   topping, divided

 2 pints vanilla ice cream

⅓ cup candy-coated
   chocolate pieces

1. Place cookies in food processor; pulse until large crumbs form. (Do not overprocess into fine crumbs.) Add ½ cup hot fudge topping; pulse just until blended. (Mixture should not be smooth; small cookie pieces may remain.)

2. Transfer mixture to pizza pan; press into even 11- to 12-inch layer about ¼ inch thick. Freeze crust 10 minutes. Meanwhile, remove ice cream from freezer to soften 10 minutes.

3. Spread ice cream evenly over crust (about ½-inch-thick layer), leaving ½-inch border. Return to freezer; freeze 2 hours or until firm.

4. Heat remaining hot fudge topping according to package directions. Drizzle over ice cream; top with chocolate pieces. Freeze 1 hour or until firm. Cut into wedges to serve.

MAKES 8 SERVINGS

CHOCOLATE CHIP SANDWICH COOKIES

¾ cup plus ⅓ cup packed brown sugar

½ cup (1 stick) butter, softened

1 egg

1 teaspoon vanilla

¾ teaspoon baking soda

½ teaspoon salt

1¾ cups all-purpose flour

3 cups semisweet chocolate chips, divided

6 tablespoons whipping cream

1. Preheat oven to 350°F. Line cookie sheets with parchment paper.

2. Beat brown sugar and butter in large bowl with electric mixer at medium speed 5 minutes or until light and fluffy. Add egg and vanilla; beat until well blended. Beat in baking soda and salt. Slowly add flour, beating at low speed until blended. Stir in 1½ cups chocolate chips. Drop heaping tablespoonfuls of dough 2 inches apart onto prepared cookie sheets.

3. Bake about 10 minutes or until cookies are just beginning to brown around edges but are still very soft in center. (Cookies will look underbaked.) Cool on cookie sheets 5 minutes. Remove to wire racks; cool completely.

4. Meanwhile for filling, bring cream to a simmer in small saucepan over medium-low heat. Place remaining 1½ cups chocolate chips in medium bowl. Pour cream over chips; let stand 1 minute. Stir until smooth. Refrigerate 1 hour, stirring occasionally. (Filling should be thick enough to spread and still be shiny when stirred.)

5. Spread heaping tablespoonful of chocolate filling onto bottoms of half of cookies. Top with remaining cookies.

MAKES 16 SANDWICH COOKIES

DOUGHNUT HOLE FONDUE

- ¾ cup whipping cream
- 1 cup bittersweet or semisweet chocolate chips
- 1 tablespoon butter
- ½ teaspoon vanilla
- 12 to 16 doughnut holes
  Sliced fresh fruit, such as pineapple, cantaloupe, strawberries and oranges

1. Heat cream in small saucepan over medium-low heat until bubbles form around edge of pan. Remove from heat. Add chocolate; let stand 2 minutes or until softened. Add butter and vanilla; whisk until smooth. Keep warm in fondue pot or transfer to serving bowl.

2. Serve with doughnut holes and fruit.

MAKES 6 SERVINGS

EASY APPLE PIE POCKETS

- 2 pieces lavash bread, each cut into 4 rectangles
- 2 tablespoons melted butter
- ¾ cup apple pie filling
- 1 egg, lightly beaten with 1 teaspoon water
- ½ cup powdered sugar
- 2½ teaspoons milk
- ⅛ teaspoon ground cinnamon

1. Preheat oven to 400°F. Line baking sheet with parchment paper.

2. Brush one side of each piece of lavash with butter. Place half of pieces on work surface buttered sides down. Spoon 3 tablespoons pie filling in center of each lavash, leaving ½-inch border. Brush border with egg wash. Top with remaining lavash pieces, buttered side up. Press edges together with tines of fork to seal. Cut three small slits in center of each pie with small knife. Place on prepared baking sheet.

3. Bake 18 minutes or until crust is golden and crisp. Remove to wire rack to cool 15 minutes.

4. Combine powdered sugar, milk and cinnamon in small bowl; whisk until smooth. Drizzle glaze over pockets; let stand 15 minutes to set.

MAKES 4 SERVINGS

COOKIE DOUGH MONKEY BREAD

1 package (about 16 ounces) refrigerated break-apart chocolate chip cookie dough (24 cookies)

2 packages (7½ ounces each) refrigerated buttermilk biscuits (10 biscuits per package)

1 cup semisweet chocolate chips, divided

¼ cup whipping cream

1. Preheat oven to 350°F. Generously spray 12-cup (10-inch) bundt pan with nonstick cooking spray.

2. Break cookie dough into 24 pieces; split each piece in half to create total of 48 pieces. Separate biscuits; cut each biscuit into four pieces with scissors. Layer half of cookie dough and half of biscuit pieces in prepared pan, alternating doughs. Sprinkle with ¼ cup chocolate chips. Repeat layers with remaining cookie dough and biscuit pieces; sprinkle with ¼ cup chocolate chips.

3. Bake 27 to 30 minutes or until biscuits are golden brown, covering pan loosely with foil during last 10 minutes of baking. Remove pan to wire rack; let stand, covered, 5 minutes. Loosen edges of bread with knife; invert onto serving plate.

4. Microwave cream in medium microwavable bowl on HIGH 1 minute or until simmering. Add remaining ½ cup chocolate chips; stir until chocolate is melted. Let stand 5 minutes to thicken slightly. Drizzle glaze over bread.

MAKES ABOUT 16 SERVINGS

CARAMEL BACON NUT BROWNIES

- ¾ cup (1½ sticks) butter
- 4 ounces unsweetened chocolate
- 2 cups sugar
- 4 eggs
- 1 cup all-purpose flour
- 1 package (14 ounces) caramels, unwrapped
- ¼ cup whipping cream
- 2 cups coarsely chopped pecans, divided
- 4 slices bacon, crisp-cooked and crumbled
- 1 package (12 ounces) chocolate chunks or chips, divided

1. Preheat oven to 350°F. Spray 13×9-inch baking pan with nonstick cooking spray.

2. Combine butter and chocolate in large microwavable bowl; microwave on HIGH 1½ to 2 minutes or until melted and smooth, stirring every 30 seconds. Stir in sugar. Add eggs, one at a time, beating until blended after each addition. Stir in flour until blended. Spread half of batter in prepared pan.

3. Bake 20 minutes. Meanwhile, combine caramels and cream in medium microwavable bowl; microwave on HIGH 1½ to 2 minutes or until caramels begin to melt. Stir until smooth. Stir in 1 cup pecans and bacon.

4. Spread caramel mixture over partially baked brownie layer. Sprinkle with half of chocolate chunks. Pour remaining brownie batter over top; sprinkle with remaining 1 cup pecans and chocolate chunks.

5. Bake 25 minutes or until set. Cool completely in pan on wire rack. Cut into squares.

MAKES 2 TO 3 DOZEN BROWNIES

CHOCOLATE CHIP COOKIE DELIGHTS

1¾ cups all-purpose flour

¾ teaspoon salt

¾ teaspoon baking powder

½ teaspoon baking soda

10 tablespoons (1¼ sticks) butter, softened

½ cup plus 2 tablespoons packed brown sugar

½ cup granulated sugar

1 egg

1 teaspoon vanilla

1½ cups semisweet or bittersweet chocolate chips

Coarse salt (optional)

Vanilla ice cream (optional)

1. Preheat oven to 375°F. Spray 18 standard (2½-inch) muffin cups with nonstick cooking spray.

2. Combine flour, ¾ teaspoon salt, baking powder and baking soda in small bowl; mix well.

3. Beat butter, brown sugar and granulated sugar in large bowl with electric mixer at medium-high speed about 5 minutes or until very light and fluffy. Add egg; beat until blended. Beat in vanilla. Stir in flour mixture until blended. Stir in chocolate chips. Spoon scant ¼ cup dough into each prepared muffin cup; sprinkle with coarse salt, if desired.

4. Bake about 14 minutes or until edges are golden brown but centers are still soft. Cool in pans 5 minutes; invert onto wire rack. Turn cookies right side up; serve warm with ice cream, if desired.

MAKES 18 SERVINGS

BACON S'MORES BUNDLES

- 1¼ cups mini marshmallows
- ¾ cup semisweet chocolate chips
- ¾ cup coarsely crushed graham crackers (5 whole graham crackers)
- 4 slices bacon, crisp-cooked and crumbled
- 1 package (about 17 ounces) frozen puff pastry, thawed

1. Preheat oven to 400°F. Combine marshmallows, chocolate chips, graham crackers and bacon in medium bowl.

2. Unfold pastry on lightly floured surface. Roll each pastry sheet into 12-inch square; cut each into four 6-inch squares. Place scant ½ cup marshmallow mixture in center of each square.

3. Brush edges of pastry squares with water. Bring edges together over filling; twist tightly to seal. Place bundles 2 inches apart on ungreased baking sheet.

4. Bake about 20 minutes or until golden brown. Cool on wire rack 5 minutes; serve warm.

MAKES 4 SERVINGS

METRIC CONVERSION CHART

VOLUME MEASUREMENTS (dry)

1/8 teaspoon = 0.5 mL
1/4 teaspoon = 1 mL
1/2 teaspoon = 2 mL
3/4 teaspoon = 4 mL
1 teaspoon = 5 mL
1 tablespoon = 15 mL
2 tablespoons = 30 mL
1/4 cup = 60 mL
1/3 cup = 75 mL
1/2 cup = 125 mL
2/3 cup = 150 mL
3/4 cup = 175 mL
1 cup = 250 mL
2 cups = 1 pint = 500 mL
3 cups = 750 mL
4 cups = 1 quart = 1 L

VOLUME MEASUREMENTS (fluid)

1 fluid ounce (2 tablespoons) = 30 mL
4 fluid ounces (1/2 cup) = 125 mL
8 fluid ounces (1 cup) = 250 mL
12 fluid ounces (1 1/2 cups) = 375 mL
16 fluid ounces (2 cups) = 500 mL

WEIGHTS (mass)

1/2 ounce = 15 g
1 ounce = 30 g
3 ounces = 90 g
4 ounces = 120 g
8 ounces = 225 g
10 ounces = 285 g
12 ounces = 360 g
16 ounces = 1 pound = 450 g

DIMENSIONS

1/16 inch = 2 mm
1/8 inch = 3 mm
1/4 inch = 6 mm
1/2 inch = 1.5 cm
3/4 inch = 2 cm
1 inch = 2.5 cm

OVEN TEMPERATURES

250°F = 120°C
275°F = 140°C
300°F = 150°C
325°F = 160°C
350°F = 180°C
375°F = 190°C
400°F = 200°C
425°F = 220°C
450°F = 230°C

BAKING PAN SIZES

Utensil	Size in Inches/Quarts	Metric Volume	Size in Centimeters
Baking or Cake Pan (square or rectangular)	8×8×2	2 L	20×20×5
	9×9×2	2.5 L	23×23×5
	12×8×2	3 L	30×20×5
	13×9×2	3.5 L	33×23×5
Loaf Pan	8×4×3	1.5 L	20×10×7
	9×5×3	2 L	23×13×7
Round Layer Cake Pan	8×1½	1.2 L	20×4
	9×1½	1.5 L	23×4
Pie Plate	8×1¼	750 mL	20×3
	9×1¼	1 L	23×3
Baking Dish or Casserole	1 quart	1 L	—
	1½ quart	1.5 L	—
	2 quart	2 L	—

192